Feasting on the Word®

WORSHIP COMPANION

ALSO AVAILABLE IN THIS SERIES

Feasting on the Word Worship Companion:
Liturgies for Year C, Volume 1

Feasting on the Word®
WORSHIP COMPANION

❧ LITURGIES FOR YEAR C ❧
VOLUME 2

EDITED BY

Kimberly Bracken Long

WJK WESTMINSTER
JOHN KNOX PRESS
LOUISVILLE · KENTUCKY

© 2013 Westminster John Knox Press

First edition

Published by Westminster John Knox Press
Louisville, Kentucky

15 16 17 18 19 20 21 22—10 9 8 7 6 5 4 3 2

Scripture quotations from the New Revised Standard Version of the Bible are copyright © 1989 by the Division of Christian Education of the National Council of the Churches of Christ in the U.S.A. and are used by permission.

Permission is granted to churches to reprint individual prayers and liturgical texts for worship provided that the following notice is included: Reprinted by permission of Westminster John Knox Press from *Feasting on the Word®* *Worship Companion.* Copyright 2013.

Book design by Drew Stevens
Cover design by Lisa Buckley and Dilu Nicholas

Library of Congress Cataloging-in-Publication Data

Feasting on the Word worship companion : liturgies for Year C / edited by Kimberly Bracken Long. — 1st ed.
    p. cm.
    Includes index.
    ISBN 978-0-664-23918-3 (v. 2 alk. paper)
    ISBN 978-0-664-23805-6 (v. 1 alk. paper)
    1. Common lectionary (1992) 2. Lectionaries. 3. Worship programs.
    I. Long, Kimberly Bracken.
    BV199.L42F43 2012
    264'.13—dc23

                                                    2012011192

PRINTED IN THE UNITED STATES OF AMERICA

∞ The paper used in this publication meets the minimum requirements
of the American National Standard for Information Sciences—Permanence of Paper
for Printed Library Materials, ANSI Z39.48-1992.

Westminster John Knox Press advocates the responsible use of our natural resources. The text paper of this book is made from 30% post-consumer waste.

Most Westminster John Knox Press books are available at special quantity discounts when purchased in bulk by corporations, organizations, and special-interest groups. For more information, please e-mail SpecialSales@wjkbooks.com.

Contents

ADDITIONAL RESOURCES

Introduction

The *Feasting on the Word Worship Companion* offers language for the church's worship for every Sunday and holy day in the Revised Common Lectionary for Years A, B, and C. This second volume provides liturgy for Year C, Trinity Sunday through Reign of Christ. It is intended to serve as a supplement to the liturgical resources of denominations and not as a substitute for any of those fine works.

The texts herein were written by people from five ecclesial bodies who share similar convictions about worship and its language, yet pray with distinct voices. Because the writers come from a range of Protestant traditions, the attentive reader will notice some differences in theological background; in every case, however, these texts are grounded in deep and careful theological reflection. We seek to offer liturgy that is accessible yet elegant, in words that are poetic but not overwrought. These texts are written for the ear; we hope they are easily spoken, and their meanings quickly apprehended, in order to encourage full and rich congregational participation in the church's life of prayer.

These words are rooted in Scripture, as the church's liturgies have been for centuries. Using the Revised Common Lectionary as a guide, the writers of this volume offer words for worship that do not merely spring from their own imaginations but are grounded in the Word of God.

What This Book Includes

— Prayers and other liturgical texts—from Opening Words to Blessing—for every Sunday and holy day from Trinity Sunday through Reign of Christ (Year C)
— A collection of greetings to be used at the beginning of a worship service

- Thanksgiving for Baptism, for use at the beginning of a worship service or for reaffirmation of baptism
- Prayers for Communion, or Eucharist
- Questions for reflection on the texts for each Sunday and holy day
- Morning and evening prayers for household use, to be prayed by individuals, families, or groups, based on the week's lectionary readings. (These prayers are written in both singular and plural, so adapt them as needed.) These may be distributed throughout a congregation for use during the week as a way to continue reflecting on the Sunday texts.
- A CD-ROM, which enables worship planners to copy text and paste it in the worship bulletin. Permission is granted to reprint individual prayers and liturgical texts for worship provided that the following notice is included: Reprinted by permission of Westminster John Knox Press from *Feasting on the Word® Worship Companion*. Copyright 2013.

Eucharistic prayers are provided in a separate section in acknowledgment that not all Christian churches celebrate the Lord's Supper every Sunday. In addition, one prayer for general use is provided along with prayers for All Saints and Reign of Christ.

How to Use This Book

One may use this book in a variety of ways. You may use the texts just as they are, or you may adapt them for your context. While new texts are offered for each Sunday, there is value in repeating portions of liturgy so that people might become familiar with them. When worshipers are able to speak the same set of words over a period of time, they are not continually adjusting to new ideas and patterns of speech. You may, for example, use the same prayer of confession for a season, allowing the people to enter more deeply into that prayer over time.

Although a basic fourfold pattern of worship is used here, the elements of worship may not be arranged in the same way they appear in your own church's order of worship. This is not intended to privilege one tradition over another, but simply to arrange the elements in a way that will look familiar to many who use this book.

You will notice that these texts are arranged in "sense lines"—that is, they look more like poems than paragraphs. This is intentional. The eye can pick up phrases quickly, enabling worshipers to pray them with greater understanding. So, if you reproduce any of these texts, please retain the sense lines.

This layout on the page also helps leaders to better speak the texts so that they can actually proclaim (and not just read) the texts, while maintaining eye contact with worshipers.

In cases where a congregational response is used, instructions are often included that will allow the prayers to be led without printing them in their entirety.

This book is full of words. Worship, however, does not happen on a page. As you use these texts, do not just read them. Pray them. Spend time with the words and make them your own so that you may lead with authenticity, wisdom, and a true sense of prayer.

A Word about the Lectionary

During Ordinary Time, or the season after Pentecost, liturgy is provided for both the semicontinuous and complementary streams of the Revised Common Lectionary. Each of these tracks uses the same epistle and gospel reading, but the Old Testament and Psalm lections are different. The semi-continuous track allows congregations to read continually through a book of Scripture from week to week. In the complementary track, the Old Testament readings are chosen to relate to (or complement) the Gospel reading of the day. In both cases, the psalm is understood as a response to the Old Testament reading. Liturgical resources for the Season after Pentecost will appear in the second volume of each year in the lectionary cycle.

Since the numbering of the Sundays after Pentecost varies from year to year, the designation of "Proper" is used here, as it is in the *Feasting on the Word* commentaries. It can be confusing to navigate the various ways churches designate Sundays; a handy resource for viewing all those labels in one place can be found at http://lectionary.library.vanderbilt.edu/, a user-friendly site provided to the public by Vanderbilt University.

Different Voices: The Ecumenical Nature of the Project

Each writer comes to his or her task having been formed by a particular liturgical tradition. We are Methodist, Episcopal, United Church of Christ, Presbyterian, and Lutheran, with a variety of backgrounds and experiences. Working as a team, we chose elements of worship that are common to all of us, as well as some elements that are particular to one church but not necessarily to another. Presbyterians, for instance, insist on including prayers of confession and prayers for illumination that invoke the Holy Spirit. Lutherans and Episcopalians expect a prayer of the day and include prayers for the departed in the intercessions. Lutherans also commonly use language about law and grace, and declarations of forgiveness sometimes refer to the ordination of the presider. These particularities were retained in order to preserve the ecumenical character of the book.

We use a variety of ways of praying but a consistent pattern of worship elements for each Sunday in the Christian year. Feel free to adapt the forms, change the words, or choose what is best suited for your context.

Who We Are

Just as this book is intended to serve as a companion to *Feasting on the Word: Preaching the Revised Common Lectionary,* we seek to be companions along the way with those of you who plan and lead worship.

The core team of writers includes:

Kimberly L. Clayton, Director of Contextual Education at Columbia Theological Seminary, Decatur, Georgia; Presbyterian Church (U.S.A.)

David Gambrell, Associate for Worship in the Office of Theology and Worship of the Presbyterian Church (U.S.A.), Louisville, Kentucky; Presbyterian Church (U.S.A.)

Daniel M. Geslin, Pastor of Sixth Avenue United Church of Christ, Denver, Colorado; United Church of Christ

Kimberly Bracken Long, Assistant Professor of Worship, Columbia Theological Seminary, Decatur, Georgia; Presbyterian Church (U.S.A.)

L. Edward Phillips, Associate Professor of Worship and Liturgical Theology, Candler School of Theology, Atlanta, Georgia; United Methodist Church

Melinda Quivik, Liturgical Scholar, Houghton, Michigan; Evangelical Lutheran Church in America

Carol L. Wade, Dean of Christ Church Cathedral, Lexington, Kentucky; Episcopal Church

Other contributors include:

Jennifer Carlier, Decatur, Georgia
Marissa Galván-Valle, Louisville, Kentucky

Kathryn Schneider Halliburton, Colorado Springs, Colorado
L'Anni Hill, Decatur, Georgia
Elizabeth C. Knowlton, Atlanta, Georgia
Franklin E. Lewis, Chester, West Virginia
Elizabeth H. Shannon, St. Petersburg, Florida
Margaret LaMotte Torrence, Asheville, North Carolina

The generosity of many people has helped bring this work to fruition. David Maxwell, executive editor of Westminster John Knox Press, has provided gentle guidance, shown great wisdom, and shared his seemingly boundless good humor. David Dobson, editorial director of WJK, has offered constant support and encouragement. Columbia Theological Seminary provided meeting space, hospitality, and encouragement for the project.

No words are sufficient to describe the depth of God's grace or beautiful enough to address to the creator of the cosmos. We offer these words with the prayer that they might be useful to the church in enabling worshiping communities to stammer forth their thanks and praise.

Kimberly Bracken Long

Trinity Sunday

Proverbs 8:1–4, 22–31   Romans 5:1–5
Psalm 8   John 16:12–15

OPENING WORDS / CALL TO WORSHIP

O Holy Trinity, One God in Three Persons,   *Ps. 8; John 16:13*
we behold in the splendor of creation
your majesty and our responsibility.
O Holy Trinity, One God in Three Persons,
we behold in the face of Jesus Christ
your divinity and our humanity.
O Holy Trinity, One God in Three Persons,
we behold in the Spirit of truth
your glory and our calling.
Bound to you forever, we will ever praise your name!
[or]
In the beginning, when God drew a circle on
the face of the deep,   *Prov. 8; John 1; Rom. 5*
Wisdom was there rejoicing, delighting
in the human race.
In the beginning was the Word, with God,
and the Word was God.
And the Word became flesh and lived among us,
full of grace and truth.
In every time and place, God's love is poured into our hearts
through the Holy Spirit that has been given to us.
Blessed are you, Father, Son, and Holy Spirit!*

*Alternate: **Blessed are you, Creator, Christ, and Holy Spirit!**

1

CALL TO CONFESSION

By faith in Jesus Christ, *Rom. 5:1–2*
we are given access to the grace of God.
Standing in that grace,
we now confess our sins before God,
seeking forgiveness and peace.

PRAYER OF CONFESSION

O Lord, our Sovereign,
how majestic is your name in all the earth.
Yet we put aside your majesty,
seeking our own power and gain.
We set aside our responsibility for the earth
entrusted to our care.
By both carelessness and design,
we pollute air, land, and waters.
In our greed, we use more resources than we rightly need.
We confess that we do not fully comprehend the damage
we have done
to the birds of the air, the creatures of the sea,
and the animals that live in forests and fields.
Forgive us, we pray.
Let your majesty fill our senses,
and pervade our actions,
that we may become better stewards of creation.
Call us, in every infant's cry,
to care for one another so that all your people flourish.
In Christ's name we pray. Amen.

[or]

Triune God,
within your own life there is mutuality, equality,
and unity in diversity.
Though we are made in your image,
we confess that we distort the triune life.
Instead of seeking mutual welfare and the common good,
we seek our own gain.
Instead of living in equality, justice, and respect,
we construct systems that are unjust.
We devise ways to elevate ourselves over others,

and disrespectful thoughts, words, and actions
    still surface in us.
We allow differences to divide us and lead to brokenness.
Holy God, forgive us.
Restore in us, and in our life together,
the divine image you intend.
Make us tender in mutuality.
Make us generous in equality.
Make us grateful in diversity.
We pray to be one with you and one another,
through Jesus Christ our Lord. Amen.

DECLARATION OF FORGIVENESS

Friends, we are still standing in the grace of Christ. *Rom. 5*
Because God's love has been poured into our hearts
    through the Holy Spirit,
we are set free to love God and neighbor,
and to work for the reconciliation of the world.
We have peace with God through our Lord Jesus Christ.
Thanks be to God!

PRAYER OF THE DAY

O God,
we honor this day
the majesty and the mystery
of your name.
You are both infinite and intimate,
known and unknowable,
transcendent and transparent.
In love, you have made us your own,
and invite us to join in your divine dance.
We will never rest until we rest in you,
Blessed Trinity,
one God forever and ever.
Amen.

PRAYER FOR ILLUMINATION

Living Word, *John 16:12–13*
you still have many things to say to us.
Speak, and we will try to bear them.

By your Word,
may the Spirit guide us into all truth,
that our lives may glorify you.
Amen.

PRAYERS OF INTERCESSION
[optional response to each intercession:]
God, in your wisdom, hear our prayer.

Holy God, you are more than we can know or name,   *Prov. 8; Rom. 5*
yet we call on you again and again
    for you alone are God.
We cannot live apart from you,
for you have called us into your triune life.
Your steadfast love surrounds us all our days.
Wherever we may be—
on a high mountain or a path in a shadowed valley,
at a crossroads on our journey,
outside the gates of welcome or in some inner circle—
you call to us,
delighting in the human race.

We come before you in thanksgiving
for all the gifts you have given that delight us so:
for the beauty of this season;
for the lives of those who bless us beyond their knowing;
for this community of faith by which we are nurtured and challenged;
for opportunities to serve you by serving others;
for goals accomplished;
and for the gift of life granted yet again today.

We come before you humbly and hopeful in need:
for those we know who are suffering today
because of illness in mind, body, or spirit;
for those trying to make a difficult decision;
for those grieving a loss, an ending, a dream deferred.
We pray for healing and strength in every broken place of our lives.
We long for the hope you alone can give—
hope that does not disappoint us
but rolls away stones of death and despair.

We pray for those whose livelihood is precarious,
for those who live at the edge of poverty's precipice,
and for those who live in temporary shelter and tenuous provision.
In the public square and in the privacy of our conscience,
help us find the will and the way toward a common good.

We come before you earnestly and urgently for this world in turmoil:
for the chaos loose in the natural world—
drought and floods, earthquakes and tornadoes—
heal the earth, we pray.
May those who are starving, thirsty,
or left in destruction's debris be restored.
We pray for the turmoil we cause
through war and violence, hatred and prejudice,
by our indifference and by our calculation.
Bring an end to our warring ways,
until civilians and soldiers live in safety and peace.
Root out of our hearts the seeds of bigotry and narrow-mindedness.
Stir us from apathy, increase in us empathy
that we may love as you love.

Holy God,
we have done so much to disrupt, disengage,
and even destroy what you have created and called good.
Still you are determined to delight in the human race.
So, make us delight-full.
Help us to delight in you by living and playing in ways that please you.
Help us to delight in neighbors near and far
by living and playing in ways that restore true communion.
Make us delightful all our days
until we greet with joy the kingdom you are bringing.
In Christ Jesus we pray. **Amen.**

INVITATION TO THE OFFERING

Out of the abundance of God's own life,
we have received the abundance of God's creation, God's word,
    and God's love.
Why, then, should we live as though we are threatened with scarcity?
Let us return to God a portion of all that we have been given,
with joyous and glad abandon.

PRAYER OF THANKSGIVING/DEDICATION

Holy God, you have poured out so much for us—
the beauty of the world,
the care of family and friends,
meaningful labor,
and the gift of the church.
We give you thanks for these and many other gifts.
Most especially,
we thank you for pouring your love
into our hearts through the Holy Spirit.
Through these offerings,
may your love spill over in glad abundance
that brings relief, renewal, and hope to those in need.
In Christ's name we pray. **Amen.**

CHARGE

Go out this day
participating in the life of the triune God—
by honoring mutuality,
living in equality and justice,
and celebrating the amazing diversity
by which our communion is enriched.

[or]

Live this day   *Rom. 5*
in patient endurance,
and stand firm in the hope that comes from God,
that others may see the glory of God
made known in Jesus Christ our Lord.

BLESSING

May the grace of Christ Jesus grant you peace;   *Rom. 5:1, 5b;*
may the Holy Spirit guide you into all truth;   *John 16:13*
and may the love of God fill your heart
so that you may find hope
in every circumstance of this life,
and give glory to God.
Amen.

Questions for Reflection

Trinity Sunday is not so much a day for explanations as it is a day for reflection on the majesty and mystery of the fullness of God: God as Creator, Lawgiver, the One who performs mighty acts; God as Messiah and Lord, Savior, Liberator, known to us in Jesus Christ; God as Holy Spirit, Wind and Flame, Advocate, Comforter. How does thinking of God in this Trinitarian way inform, even increase, your understanding of God? Do you experience God, or relate more easily to God, in one of the three "Persons" of God more than the other two? What causes you to relate to God more closely in this way?

Household Prayer: Morning

Creator God, I wake this morning to the beauty of the world
as though it were the first morning of creation.
As the light of the sun rises on all that you have made,
I pray that my spirit may rise also.
Help me to be ready to greet you
however and in whomever you make yourself known to me today.
Help me to pause in moments of this day
to glimpse the beauty you have made,
offered as gift and sign of your abiding presence.
I entrust myself and those I love to you this day,
knowing that you promise to be with us always.
In your holy, triune name I pray. Amen.

Household Prayer: Evening

O God, my Advocate and Comforter, I rest in you.
The evening falls and the darkness does not overcome me,
for you are my light.
You are the Light of the world.
I bring to you the passing cares of this day,
and the deeper cares of my life and those I love.
Breathe peace on all that stirs in me and whirls around me.
Breathe peace into every troubled place and person this night.
Shine on us, in us, and through us.
I know that when I awake, I will still be with you,
Holy One who is Source, Word, and Wisdom. Amen.

Proper 3

(Sunday between May 22 and May 28 inclusive)

Sirach 27:4–7 *or* Isaiah 55:10–13   1 Corinthians 15:51–58
Psalm 92:1–4, 12–15   Luke 6:39–49

CALL TO WORSHIP / OPENING WORDS
It is good to give thanks to you, O Lord.   *Ps. 92:1–2*
We declare your steadfast love in the morning.
It is good to sing praises to your name.
We proclaim your faithfulness by night.
For you, O Lord, have made us glad by your work;
at the work of your hands we sing for joy!
[or]
Like people long in exile, we look to God
        for hope.   *Isa. 55:11; Luke 6:45*
Your word, O God, is not empty;   *1 Cor. 15:51–52*
it is full and accomplishes your purpose.
We open the treasure of our heart, asking God to fill us.
Your word, O God, is not empty;
it is full and accomplishes your purpose.
In the mystery of life and death, we listen attentively.
Your word, O God, is not empty;
it is full and accomplishes your purpose.

CALL TO CONFESSION
[Reader 1:] As a tree is known by its fruit,   *Luke 6:44–45*
[Reader 2:] so we are known by our words.
[Reader 1:] We are known by our words
[Reader 2:] for it is out of the abundance of the heart
        that the mouth speaks.
[Reader 1:] Let us confess the brokenness that is in our hearts
        and our speech.
[or]

8

As fruit discloses the cultivation of a tree, *Sir. 27:6*
so our conversation discloses the cultivation of our minds.
Let us confess what our words disclose.

[or]

As our physical bodies carry the scars
   of past falls and injuries, *1 Cor. 15:53–54, 57*
we also carry scars in our minds and hearts:
Memories can sting when we remember
falling short of our best intentions.
The knowledge of injuries we have caused,
intentionally and unintentionally,
overpowers us.
As we confess our sins to God,
we also confess our faith in God's victory over sin and death
through Jesus Christ our Lord.

PRAYER OF CONFESSION

God of mercy, *Sir. 27:5*
as the kiln tests the potter's handiwork,
so we are tested by our words.

When we use our words to judge—rather than to engage,
Lord, have mercy.
When we use our words to incite violence—rather than to build peace,
Lord, have mercy.
When we use our words to disperse—rather than to gather,
Lord, have mercy.
When we use our words because we are afraid to use our hands,
Lord, have mercy.
When we use our words because we are afraid to open our hearts,
Lord, have mercy.
Christ, have mercy.
Lord, have mercy.

[or]

O God our Rock, in you there is *Ps. 92:15b;*
   no unrighteousness, *Luke 6:41–49*
but we have sinned against you and our neighbor.
We call upon your name and then go our own way,
apart from your purposes.

We are quick to see the fault in others,
but do not see our own failings.
Forgive us, we pray, for any haughtiness or hypocrisy in us.
Correct our hearts, we pray,
that we may correct our mouths and our actions.
Forgive us for putting our trust in shallow things,
and give us faith to trust the sure foundation you have established.
We pray in the name of the One
who sees us clearly and loves us well, Jesus the Christ. Amen.

DECLARATION OF FORGIVENESS

Out of a heart of abundance God spoke,   *Luke 6:45; John 1:14; 12:47*
and the Word came into the world.
And the Word became flesh
and lived among us,
not to judge us
but to save us.
Believe the gospel.
In Jesus Christ, we are forgiven.

[or]

Because Jesus Christ has been raised from the dead,   *1 Cor. 15:54*
sin and death have been swallowed up.
God's victory over every destructive power is assured.
This is the good news upon which we stand:
In Jesus Christ, we are forgiven.

PRAYER OF THE DAY

Spirit of God,
ever-present companion,
may your constant presence
ignite in us
a carefree courage
that we may boldly take part in your kingdom. **Amen.**

[or]

God Most High,   *Ps. 92:2–3, 13–14; 1 Cor. 15:52–53*
at the sound of the lute and harp,
we awake to sing your praises.
At the sound of the last trumpet,
we will awake to praise you forever.
Whether we are young or old,

we want to flourish in your presence
until all that you intend is fulfilled.
Then our praises, like our bodies,
will be imperishable before you,
Eternal One.
Amen.

PRAYER FOR ILLUMINATION

Spirit of God,   *Isa. 55:10*
may your Word be as rain
falling from heaven, soaking dry soil
until it sprouts and springs forth,
giving seed to the sower
and bread to the eater,
through Christ—
Living Water, Living Word. **Amen.**

[or]

O God,   *Isa. 55:10–11*
as rain and snow fall from heaven,
your word now falls upon us.
May it produce good seed in us,
becoming bread for a hungry world.
By the power of the Holy Spirit,
may your word never return to you empty.
In us, even in us, may your word
accomplish your purpose.
We ask it in Christ's name. **Amen.**

PRAYERS OF INTERCESSION

[Allow ample time for silent prayer.]
Creator God, you spoke the world into being.   *John 1:14; Rom. 8:26*
Impart your creative wisdom to our leaders,
that by their words they may do your will.
[silent prayer]

Jesus Christ, you are the living Word.
Enliven our conversation,
that through our words all may know you.
[silent prayer]

Holy Spirit, you speak with sighs too deep for words.
Intercede when our words fail us,
that by your groans we may receive healing.
[silent prayer]
This we pray in the strong name of the triune God.
Amen.

[or]

God of steadfast love and faithfulness,   *Ps. 92:2, 13; Isa. 55:12–13;*
here in your house, gathered in the company   *1 Cor. 15:57*
    of your people,
we flourish in your presence.
We hear your words of life and hope,
and we are strengthened in joy.
As you led your people out of exile long ago,
so you continue to lead us home to you in paths of peace.
We give you thanks and praise, O God.

Because we know how quickly things can change in this life,
in a moment, in the twinkling of an eye,
we pause to offer our prayers of petition:

We name before you those who are in need of healing from illness:
those newly diagnosed;
those who endure chronic pain;
those in recovery, whether long or short.
Grant strength and healing to them
and uphold all who care for them:
doctors and nurses, families and friends . . . *[silence is kept]*

We name before you those in need of comfort and encouragement:
to one weighed down by grief,
bring the light and peace of your presence;
to one burdened by worries over a relationship, employment,
    or responsibilities,
grant courage and grace . . . *[silence is kept]*

We also bring to you, O God, our joys and celebrations.
We give you thanks for opportunities for rest and play;
for glad reunions bringing laughter and joy;

for special celebrations of birthdays, anniversaries,
and other milestones reached in our lives.
We thank you for new beginnings.
We are grateful even for "ordinary" days,
in which family members and friends grace us
in casual, even unseen ways . . . *[silence is kept]*

Our prayers are never for ourselves alone.
We name before you the cares and needs
in our community and in your wider world:
For those who do not have enough to eat,
or clean water to drink,
or a place to call home,
we pray that you will increase in us and others
generosity enough to share resources in life-giving ways.

We pray for those caught in the danger of war.
Bring an end to our warring ways.
In place of the thorn, make a cypress to grow;
in place of a brier, cause the myrtle to bloom;
in place of our hatred and fear,
sow the seeds of love and understanding.
Keep us from ostracizing
and consigning some people into places of exile and exclusion.
Teach us instead to build community across many divides
until every person is free to come and go in joy and peace.

All these prayers we offer with the confidence of children,
knowing that in Jesus Christ the victory has been won
over death and every other power that destroys.
We pray in the name of him
who reigns with you in highest heaven, Jesus Christ our Lord. **Amen.**

INVITATION TO THE OFFERING

It is good to give thanks to the Lord,   *Ps. 92:1–2*
to declare God's steadfast love in the morning,
and God's faithfulness by night.
Let us proclaim our trust in God's faithfulness
by giving our tithes and offerings.
[or]

Psalm 92 is the only one in the Psalter
assigned to a particular day—the Sabbath day.
In Sabbath rest from our labors,
we are invited to consider and give thanks
for the wonderful works of God's hands.
On this Sabbath day, our hands are freed
to give back to God our praise
and this offering of all we have so generously received.

PRAYER OF THANKSGIVING/DEDICATION

Creator of abundance, *Matt. 6:10*
Spirit of wisdom,
may you use the gifts of the church and the gifts of our lives
that your kingdom may come
and your will be done
through Christ, Lord of extravagant love. **Amen.**

[or]

Gracious and generous God, *Isa. 55:12–13*
you are with us always, providing for our needs.
Even when we seem far from you,
you lead us back, offering joy and peace.
No less than the mountains and hills,
we will burst into songs of praise.
No less than the trees of the field,
we will clap our hands in thanksgiving.
No less, no less;
for you deserve all that we have and all that we are.
Receive what we have brought today:
our tithes, our prayers, and our praise,
signs of our dedication to you.
In Christ's name, we pray. **Amen.**

CHARGE

Beloved, go out in joy; *Isa. 55:12; 1 Cor. 15:58*
be steadfast,
immovable,
always excelling in the work of the Lord;
and be led back in peace,
because you know that in the Lord
your labor is not in vain.

[or]

Beloved,   *1 Cor. 15:58*
be steadfast, immovable,
always excelling in the work of the Lord,
because you know that whatever you do
in accord with God
is never done in vain.

[or]

Go out in joy,   *Isa. 55:12; Ps. 92:4*
be led in peace,
giving praise to the God who makes you glad
    all your days.

BLESSING

May the Lord bless you and keep you.   *Num. 6:24–26*
May the Lord's face shine with love upon you,
    and be gracious to you.
May the Lord's presence be always with you
    and give you peace.

[or]

May God, our Rock, be your sure foundation in
    every storm.   *Ps. 92:15b; Luke 6:49*
May Christ, our Savior, be your victory over
    sin and death.   *1 Cor. 15:57*
May the Holy Spirit, our Helper, be your guide in
    every time of need.   *John 14:16, 26*

Questions for Reflection

What would my conversation sound like if I were to cultivate the mind of
Christ from morning through nightfall?

[or]

Luke 6:39–49 is the concluding section of Jesus' Sermon on the Plain. The
sermon begins with a series of blessings and woes, then calls us to love
our enemies, not to judge others, to forgive and show mercy, as God has
shown mercy to us. Jesus then uses exaggeration to help us see how far we
are from the faithful life God intends. Jesus says we are more concerned
about the speck in our neighbor's eye than the log sticking out of our own
eye. What "log" impedes you from being the person you want to be? What

"logjam" in your heart, mind, or actions would you like to whittle down, freeing you to be more Christlike?

Household Prayer: Morning

Lord, your love is like a river, *Ps. 92:1–2*
steadfast and forever.
Open wide my soul
that your love may overflow into my life today
and cover all I meet;
through Christ whose love is never ending. Amen.

[or]

Dear God, this morning the day is bright with promise. *Luke 6*
As the sun brings clarity to the contours of my room
    and the world outside,
so shine your light upon the contours of my life and habits.
Grant clarity so that I may pay attention to the ways
    I interact with others.
Help me to show love and mercy to all
    according to the measure of their need.
Clear my eyes so that I may see you in unexpected ways today.
Then, in your mercy, grant me grace
as I learn to love others as you love me.
In Christ's name, I pray. Amen.

Household Prayer: Evening

Lord, *Ps. 92:1–2*
your faithfulness to me is never ending.
Grant me peace to close my eyes,
and put my thoughts and fears to rest,
knowing I will awake again
to your steadfast love in the morning;
through Christ whose faithfulness is never ending. Amen.

[or]

God my Rock and my Rest,   *Luke 6; Ps. 92*
thank you for the gift of the day as it has been.
For every opportunity you gave me
to understand someone better today, I thank you.
For every opportunity you gave me
to understand myself better today, I also give you thanks.
I still need to forgive _____,
and I pray that you will help me move toward generosity
     in that relationship.
Now, O Lord, grant me rest and sleep.
Thank you that you never sleep,
but watch over the whole creation in steadfast love and faithfulness. Amen.

Proper 4

(Sunday between May 29 and June 4 inclusive)

SEMICONTINUOUS

1 Kings 18:20–21 (22–29), 30–39   Galatians 1:1–12
Psalm 96   Luke 7:1–10

OPENING WORDS / CALL TO WORSHIP
Worship the Lord in holy splendor.   *Ps. 96*
Tremble before God, all the earth.
Highest heavens,
be glad!
Widest earth,
rejoice!
Mighty waters,
shout your praise!
Forests and fields,
sing for joy!
The Lord is coming to judge the earth,
with equity and strength,
with righteousness and truth.
The Lord is coming to judge the earth.
The Lord is coming to reign in glory.
[or]
Choose this day whom you will serve.   *Deut. 6; Josh. 24;*
The Lord is our God, the Lord alone.   *1 Kgs. 18; Ps. 96*
Cry aloud, and call upon God's name.
The Lord is our God, the Lord alone.
Declare God's glory among the nations.
The Lord is our God, the Lord alone.
Sing to the Lord, and bless God's name.
The Lord is our God, the Lord alone.

CALL TO CONFESSION

Hear now the first commandment: *Exod. 20:1–3*
"You shall have no other gods before me," says
    the Lord.
But we do have other gods
that claim our adoration,
our time, our energy,
our resources, our hearts.
Let us confess our idolatry,
trusting in God's mercy to save.

PRAYER OF CONFESSION

When we limp around altars we have made   *1 Kgs. 18:26–29*
    with anxious expectation of idols we adore,
    Lord, have mercy.

When we whip ourselves with condemnation,
    sacrificing our very selves for that which cannot satisfy,
    Lord, bring healing.

When we beg our idols to meet our deepest need—
    and there is
    no voice,
    no answer,
    no response
    Lord, save us! Amen.

DECLARATION OF FORGIVENESS

[While pouring water into the font, the liturgist proclaims:]
The Lord Jesus Christ poured out his very self   *Gal. 1:4, 5:1*
to set us free from the idols that enslave us!

*[Liturgist scoops water with hands, lifted high with joy to scatter
droplets toward congregation:]*
It is for freedom that Christ has set us free!
Stand firm, then, and do not let yourselves be burdened again
    by a yoke of slavery.

PRAYER OF THE DAY

We are like foreigners, O God, *1 Kgs. 8:41–43*
who have come from a distant land
because of your great name,
because of your mighty hand, your outstretched arm.
Enfold us now, O God,
not as strangers, but as beloved children. **Amen.**

PRAYER FOR ILLUMINATION

Lord, as we hear your word proclaimed *Gal. 1:11–12*
may it be for us truly good news,
a gospel not of human origin,
but a revelation given through Jesus Christ,
made alive to us through your Holy Spirit. **Amen.**

PRAYERS OF INTERCESSION

Lord, it is hard to have faith in our broken world, *Luke 7:1–10*
where illness, disaster, and corruption
    threaten to claim authority.

But you are the ultimate authority, O God,
so we boldly come before you in faith to lift up
    our concerns:
For those who are sick, crushed and enslaved,
    we beseech you:
Come, Lord, and heal.

For those deadened by daily drudgery,
Come, Lord, and enliven.

For the leaders of our community, our town, our nation,
Come, Lord, and guide.

For those on the margins, the unnoticed and the unloved,
Come, Lord, and embrace.

For those imprisoned, whether behind bars of steel
    or behind hearts of stone,
Come, Lord, and redeem.

For those at the end of their lives,
Come, Lord, and eternally enfold.

In the name of Jesus, who prays for us.
Amen.

INVITATION TO THE OFFERING

Ascribe to the Lord the glory due God's name. *Ps. 96:8*
O people, with cheerful hearts
bring your offering into the courts of God!

PRAYER OF THANKSGIVING/DEDICATION

Lord of all we have and all we are,
what we offer here has been blessed by your
    supreme goodness.
With these offerings now bless others
that they too may know
that you are Lord of all they have and all they are;
In Jesus' name. **Amen.**

CHARGE

Brothers and sisters, *Gal. 1:10*
seek not to please others;
seek rather the approval of God alone.
Go now in peace,
    and with your lives preach the gospel.

BLESSING

Grace to you and peace *Gal. 1:3–5*
from God who has made us,
Christ who redeems us,
and the Spirit who sustains us,
to whom be glory forever and ever. **Amen.**

Question for Reflection

What "gods" claim my allegiance today?

Household Prayer: Morning

Spirit of life,
may we breathe in your holiness—
 deeply, deeply—
 until every cell is filled
and we become wholly yours,
every breath a new song. Amen.

Household Prayer: Evening

Spirit of life,
as the shadows lengthen and the daylight fades,
may we again become quiet,
your Holy Breath living and moving within us,
a gentle reminder
that even when we forget our breath
it continues,
keeping us alive. Amen.

Proper 4

(Sunday between May 29 and June 4 inclusive)

COMPLEMENTARY

1 Kings 8:22–23, 41–43   Galatians 1:1–12
Psalm 96:1–9   Luke 7:1–10

OPENING WORDS / CALL TO WORSHIP
Lord, you are sovereign!   *Ps. 96*
[Men:] **The seas roar!**
[Women:] **The fields exult!**

All the trees of the forest sing for joy
in anticipation of your holy presence.
We long to belong to your joyful kingdom, O God!
Reveal the power of your majesty to us
as our voices join the ongoing song of creation's praise.
[or]
Worship the Lord in holy splendor.   *Ps. 96*
Tremble before God, all the earth.
Highest heavens,
be glad!
Widest earth,
rejoice!
Mighty waters,
shout your praise!
Forests and fields,
sing for joy!
The Lord is coming to judge the earth,
with equity and strength,
with righteousness and truth.
The Lord is coming to judge the earth.
The Lord is coming to reign in glory.

CALL TO CONFESSION

By the grace of Jesus Christ   *Gal. 1:2*
we are beloved children of God,
members of God's own family.
With the confidence of beloved children,
let us confess our sin.

PRAYER OF CONFESSION

O Lord our God, we confess to you   *1 Kgs. 18; Ps. 96; Gal. 1;*
our unfaithfulness,   *Luke 7*
our divided loyalties,
our dancing around the truth.
We look for human approval
instead of seeking to serve you.
We answer to human authority
instead of listening for your Word.
Turn our hearts back to you.
Consume our sin with holy fire
and set us free to sing your praise. Amen.

DECLARATION OF FORGIVENESS

This is the gospel,   *Gal. 1:4, 6–7*
the good news we have received:
that our Lord Jesus Christ loves us
and gave his life
to set us free from our sins.
Hear the good news!
In Jesus Christ we are forgiven.
Thanks be to God.

PRAYER OF THE DAY

Holy God, we are not worthy   *Luke 7*
to enter into your house.
Only speak your saving Word,
that you may find faith in us
when Christ returns in glory. **Amen.**

PRAYER FOR ILLUMINATION

O Lord, by the gift of your Holy Spirit,   *Gal. 1*
let us hear the good news of the gospel,

words not of human origin,
but a message of grace
revealed to us through Jesus Christ,
your Word made flesh. **Amen.**

PRAYERS OF INTERCESSION

Answer us, O Lord; *1 Kgs. 18*
hear our prayers when we call upon your name.

[optional response to each intercession:]
Only say the word, Lord,
and all shall be well. *Luke 7:7*

For your church,
that we may be faithful in following you
and telling the good news of the gospel. *Gal. 1*

For all nations and peoples,
that you would bring an end to violence
and the conflicts that divide us. *1 Kgs. 18*

For the earth you have made,
that the seas and skies, forests and fields
would show your goodness and glory. *Ps. 96*

For all who are ill or close to death,
that you would heal the sick
and bring peace to the dying. *Luke 7*

O Lord our God,
as we lift our hearts and hands to heaven,
reach out to us in mercy
with your outstretched arm.
This we pray in the name
of Jesus Christ our Lord. **Amen.** *1 Kgs. 8*

INVITATION TO THE OFFERING

Let us give glory to the name of the Lord *Ps. 96:8*
by offering our lives to God
in thanksgiving and praise.

.

PRAYER OF THANKSGIVING/DEDICATION

O Lord our God, there is no one like you   *1 Kgs. 8*
in heaven above or on the earth below.
You are faithful to your promises,
showing steadfast love to your people.
Receive this offering of our lives
as a sacrifice of thanksgiving and praise.
Let our lives show forth to all the world
the glory of your holy name. **Amen.**

CHARGE

Sing to the Lord a new song!   *Ps. 96:1–2*
Tell everyone about God's saving love
this day and every day.

BLESSING

Grace and peace to you   *Gal. 1*
from God our Father
and the Lord Jesus Christ.
To God be the glory forever!

Questions for Reflection

In Luke 7:1–10 Jesus praises the faith of a centurion, who trusts in the
authority of Jesus' word to heal. In Galatians 1:1–12, Paul insists that the
authority of the gospel comes from its source in the revelation of Jesus
Christ, not of human origin. What does authority have to do with faith?
Who are the authorities you trust, and why? Who are the authorities you
don't trust, and why not?

Household Prayer: Morning

Lord God,
we sing a new song of praise to you
for the gift of this new day.
By your grace and truth, make us ready
to sing with the heavens and the earth
when you come again in glory;
through Jesus Christ our Savior. Amen.

Household Prayer: Evening

God of faithfulness and steadfast love,
hold us in your mighty hand this night
and stretch out your arm to shelter us.
Let this home be your dwelling place
and let your house be our eternal rest. Amen.

Proper 5

SEMICONTINUOUS

1 Kings 17:8–16 (17–24)   Galatians 1:11–24
Psalm 146   Luke 7:11–17

OPENING WORDS / CALL TO WORSHIP

Praise the Lord!   *Ps. 146:1–2*
Praise the Lord, O my soul!
Lord, we will praise you as long as we live!
[or]
Praise the Lord!   *Ps. 146*
I will praise the Lord as long as I live.
Sing praises to God,
who made heaven and earth,
who is faithful forever,
who gives justice to the oppressed,
who gives food to the hungry,
who sets the prisoners free,
who watches over the stranger,
who cares for widows and orphans.
The Lord will reign forever.
Praise the Lord!

CALL TO CONFESSION

Happy are those whose hope is in the Lord their God,   *Ps. 146:5, 8*
who lifts up those who are bowed down.
Let us humble ourselves and confess our sin.

PRAYER OF CONFESSION

Lord, forgive us.
We are blind to our own brokenness,
yet focused on the failings of others.

We are deaf to the cries of those who need us,
numb to the need of those who hurt.
We are silent when words are needed,
impotent when action is required.
Lord, hear our anguish,
pity our brokenness,
speak life and forgiveness
to our weary souls. Amen.

DECLARATION OF FORGIVENESS

Beloved, hear the good news: *Ps. 146:5–6*
through Christ we are forgiven!
Our hope is in the Lord our God,
who keeps faith with us forever.
God's mercy is everlasting!

PRAYER OF THE DAY

Gracious God,   *Luke 7*
draw near to us with compassion,
touch us with healing,
and speak to us with love,
so that we may arise and live
to spread the good news
of your saving power;
through Jesus Christ our Lord. **Amen.**

PRAYER FOR ILLUMINATION

Holy God,   *Gal. 1:15–16*
enlighten us by your Holy Spirit,
and reveal yourself to us,
that we may hear your word
and proclaim your good news in the world. **Amen.**
[or]
Speak to us, O Lord,   *1Kgs. 17*
your saving Word;
fill us with your Holy Spirit
and feed us with the bread of life. **Amen.**
[or]

Gracious God, by your Holy Spirit,   *1 Kgs. 17:24*
may the words of my mouth be true,
the thoughts of my heart be pure,
and the ways of my life be love;
for the sake of the Lord Jesus Christ. **Amen.**

PRAYERS OF INTERCESSION
[Allow ample time for silent prayer.]
Let us pray for the world, saying,   Ps. 146:5–9; 1 Kgs. 17:21
Lord we pray,
let your life fill this child again.

Breath of life,
breathe into us,
that we might live.

For the one who is bowed down
by the weight of what cannot be controlled . . . .
[silent prayer]
Lord, we pray,
let your life fill this child again.

For the one who is blinded
by the shimmer of insatiable desires . . .
[silent prayer]
Lord, we pray,
let your life fill this child again.

For the one who is hopeless,
helpless, lost in fear . . .
[silent prayer]
Lord, we pray,
let your life fill this child again.

For the one who is imprisoned,
abandoned, left to die . . .
[silent prayer]
Lord, we pray,
let your life fill this child again.

For the one who is preparing
to leave this home on earth . . .
[silent prayer]
Lord, we pray,
let your life fill this child forever and ever.

All these prayers we offer to you, O God,
through Jesus Christ who prays for us
and the Holy Spirit who intercedes for us
in sighs too deep for words. **Amen.**

INVITATION TO THE OFFERING

Happy are those whose help is the God of Jacob,   *Ps. 146:5*
whose hope is in the Lord their God.
Let us proclaim our trust in the Lord
by giving our tithes and offerings.

PRAYER OF THANKSGIVING/DEDICATION

Lord, may others glorify you because of
    these offerings,   *Gal. 1:24*
given in Jesus' name. **Amen.**

CHARGE

Beloved, you were set apart before you were born.   *Gal. 1:15–16*
You were called through God's grace.
Go out now in joy and with your lives proclaim
    this gospel!

BLESSING

And now, may the Lord bless you, keep you, and
    enfold you in love.
Amen.

Question for Reflection

Psalm 146 describes God's care for widows and orphans, an important
biblical theme. 1 Kings 17:17–24 and Luke 7:11–17 tell how the son of a
widow is restored to life by the power of God. How does the church show
God's favor to those who are most vulnerable? How do we proclaim the
hope of the resurrection to those who have been touched by death?

Household Prayer: Morning

Lord, as I awake
to the light of this day
May I reflect your light
in every moment
and speak forth your praise
with every breath. Amen

Household Prayer: Evening

Lord, when I feel orphaned,   *Ps. 146:9*
motherless,
fatherless,
or simply less,
I am grateful
that you hold me close. Amen.

Proper 5

(Sunday between June 5 and June 11 inclusive)

COMPLEMENTARY

1 Kings 17:17–24	Galatians 1:11–24
Psalm 30	Luke 7:11–17

OPENING WORDS / CALL TO WORSHIP

Sing praise to the Lord, you faithful people.   *Ps. 30*
Give thanks to God's holy name.
For the Lord restores our life;
God raises us from the dead.
Will the dust sing God's praise,
or tell of God's faithfulness?
Our souls will sing to the Lord.
How can we be silent?
We will give thanks to God forever.

CALL TO CONFESSION

God's anger is but for a moment;   *Ps. 30:5*
God's favor is for a lifetime.
Trusting in God's grace, let us confess our sin.

PRAYER OF CONFESSION

Loving God, hear our prayer—   *Ps. 30*
our eyes are tired from weeping,
our hearts are heavy with sin.

We have trusted too much in our own strength.
We have hidden our faces from those who suffer.
We have turned away from neighbors in need.
We have given up hope instead of seeking your help.

Lord, be gracious to us.
Forgive our sin,

heal our brokenness,
and fill our hearts with songs of joy. Amen.

DECLARATION OF FORGIVENESS

Weeping may linger for the night, *Ps. 30:5*
but joy comes with the morning.
Hear the good news!
In Jesus Christ we are forgiven.
Thanks be to God.

PRAYER OF THE DAY

O Lord God, *Ps. 30*
who dances away our mourning
and clothes us with joy,
linger with us in our weeping
and stay throughout the night,
that having walked within the darkness,
we may embrace the coming light
when your joy comes in the morning
and overtakes the dark of night. **Amen.**
[or]
Gracious God, *Luke 7*
draw near to us with compassion,
touch us with healing,
and speak to us with love,
so that we may arise and live
to spread the good news
of your saving power;
through Jesus Christ our Lord. **Amen.**

PRAYER FOR ILLUMINATION

Holy God, *Gal. 1:15–16*
enlighten us by your Holy Spirit,
and reveal yourself to us,
that we may hear your Word
and proclaim your good news to the world. **Amen.**
[or]
Speak to us, O Lord, *1 Kgs. 17*
your saving Word;

fill us with your Holy Spirit
and feed us with the bread of life. **Amen.**

PRAYERS OF INTERCESSION

We cry to you for help, O Lord,
for you alone have the power to restore our lives.

[optional response to each intercession:]
Hear us, O Lord,
be gracious to us.   *Ps. 30:10*

Give bread to those who are hungry
and drink to those who thirst.   *1 Kgs. 17*

Give life to those who are dying
and grace to those who are sick with sin.   *1 Kgs.17; Luke 7*

Give justice to those who are oppressed
and peace to those who live in fear.   *Gal. 1*

Give comfort to those who mourn
and hope to those who despair.   *1 Kgs. 17; Ps. 30; Luke 7*

As you breathe life into dust
and make dry bones dance with joy,
give new life to this weary world;
through Jesus Christ our Savior. **Amen.**   *Gen. 2; Ps. 30; Ezek. 37*

INVITATION TO THE OFFERING

God calls us to share what we have—   *I Kgs. 17*
a little bread, a little water—
and God uses those simple gifts
to bring abundant blessing to the world.

PRAYER OF THANKSGIVING/DEDICATION

Thanks and praise to you, O God;   *1 Kgs. 17; Luke 7*
by your grace you bring the dead to life.
Let us use the breath you have given us
to speak your truth and sing your glory;
through Jesus Christ our Lord. **Amen.**

CHARGE

> Your life is a gift of grace; *1 Kgs. 17; Gal. 1; Luke 7*
> use it to give glory to God!

BLESSING

> Now arise and go with joy! *Luke 7:11–17*
> God looks with favor upon you.

Questions for Reflection

Where do you need God's breath of life?

Household Prayer: Morning

We give you thanks, O God,
for it is by the gift of your grace
that we rise from our beds each morning.
Keep us in your grace this day
so that we may rise to give you thanks
on the morning of your new creation;
through Jesus Christ our Lord. Amen.

Household Prayer: Evening

Our trust is in you, O God, in you alone—
for you have given us life and breath,
food to satisfy our hunger,
and faith to nourish our souls.
Watch over us this night,
uphold us by your strength,
and keep us in your way,
so that we may praise your name
as long as we live. Amen.

Proper 6

(Sunday between June 12 and June 18 inclusive)

SEMICONTINUOUS

1 Kings 21:1–10 (11–14), 15–21a   Galatians 2:15–21
Psalm 5:1–8   Luke 7:36–8:3

OPENING WORDS / CALL TO WORSHIP
In the morning, O Lord, you hear our prayers.   *Ps. 5*
In the light of this day we praise your name.
Through the abundance of your steadfast love
you have gathered us into your house.
In the holiness of your presence,
we bow down to worship and adore you.

CALL TO CONFESSION
The God of the oppressed hunts evil as a lioness stalks prey,
so that sin cannot hide in high or low places.
But the Holy One also forgives all who repent.
Let us confess our sins.

PRAYER OF CONFESSION
God of justice and mercy,
we confess that we disobey your will.
We show neither justice nor mercy to others.

Christ our Savior, love incarnate,
we confess that we take your love for granted.
We do not give of ourselves,
nor do we rejoice in all the blessings we receive.

Holy Spirit, power and breath,
we confess that we block your movement.
We do not live holy lives
of sacrificial love.

**Gracious Trinity, forgive us
and grant us your peace.
Help us to turn from our sins
so that we may love you
by joyfully caring for others. Amen.**

DECLARATION OF FORGIVENESS

Jesus said to the one who had sinned much, *Luke 7:48*
"Your sins are forgiven."

The cross of Christ stands as the sign
that the love of God lives in us
through faith in the grace of God.

In the power of the Christ's Spirit, I say to you,
your sins are forgiven.

PRAYER OF THE DAY

God of all nations,
your just rule is the measure of every law,
and your compassion instructs every ruler.
May the people of the earth
heed the call of your prophets for justice and kindness,
and may all trust your love
revealed in the cross of our Lord, Jesus Christ. **Amen.**

PRAYER FOR ILLUMINATION

Holy One,
when your prophets speak justice by the Spirit,
the powerless clap their hands.
When your Son declares forgiveness,
sinners cry tears of joy.

By the power of your Holy Spirit,
open our ears to your word
and move our hearts to respond in ways that honor you;
in the name of Jesus Christ, our Lord. **Amen.**

PRAYERS OF INTERCESSION

Almighty God,

you love what you create.
We pray for the earth,
that its air, soil, and water
be refreshed and restored to health.

We pray for all your creatures,
that, as the community of life,
we may share fairly the harvests
of land and sea.

We pray for all nations and people.
Let us share the riches of our cultures
without hatred or fear or suspicion.

We pray for all who govern.
Grant a spirit of wisdom, compassion, and courage
to those in authority
whom you charge with the tasks
of leading and safeguarding others.

We pray for the poor and the sick,
the weak and the vulnerable.
Be their protector, healer, and vindicator,
easing the sufferings of body, mind, and spirit.

We pray for the church.
Strengthen the body of Christ
with the Holy Spirit,
so that we have the mind of Christ among us.

Equip your people to serve with love
the world you sent your Son to save.
May our ministry take the form of his cross,
as we proclaim his resurrection,
and look forward to his coming in glory. **Amen.**

INVITATION TO THE OFFERING

An unnamed woman went to a Pharisee's home   *Luke 7:36–8:3*
to worship Jesus in thanks for her new life.
Like her, Christ sets us free

with gifts of mercy, grace, and love.
Our sins are forgiven, and our lives are made whole.
Let us pour out our thanksgivings before God.

PRAYER OF THANKSGIVING/DEDICATION

Holy Trinity of love,
God of heaven and earth,
you pour down justice
like a rushing mountain stream;
you raise mercy and kindness
like a new day dawning.
We thank you for creating this good planet,
and for the your care of all that dwell here.
We thank you for our lives redeemed and made new
by the life, death, and resurrection of Jesus Christ.
We thank you for his holy rule
that promises your peaceable reign
in our homes, in our nation, and among all nations.
We thank you for the power given through Christ
to forgive others as we have been forgiven.
We present our tithes and offerings in joyful thanksgiving
for all the blessings we have received from you.
Use them and us as instruments of your peace,
serving the call of the church,
until Christ comes in final victory. **Amen.**

CHARGE

Be fair and just in everything you do.
Forgive those who do you wrong.
Be merciful and kind,
especially to those who are weaker than you.
Be guided by the cross of Jesus Christ,
who is your judge and your salvation.

BLESSING

You are made in the image of God,
saved by the Son of God,
given life and faith by the Spirit of God.
The triune God loves you, and will forever.
Go in peace. **Amen.**

Question for Reflection

What is the relationship between justice and forgiveness in a Christian's life?

Household Prayer: Morning

Holy One, Holy Three,
be my guide, my guardian, and my strength today.
Let me be treated fairly by all whom I meet,
and remind me to treat fairly all whom I meet.
Grant me Christ's forgiveness from anyone I harm,
and charge me in Christ's name
to forgive anyone who does me harm.
So, guide my ways,
guard my life,
and grant me strength
to honor the crucified Son,
Holy Three, Holy One. Amen.

Household Prayer: Evening

Eternal God,
as this day comes to a close,
I thank you for every blessing
I have received.
Forgive me for the wrongs I have done
and the good I have neglected.
Grant me rest in your arms,
free of regret and worry.
Let sleep restore and refresh me,
so that I may rise to a new day,
giving you thanks and praise
by the power of the Holy Spirit,
in the name of Jesus Christ. Amen.

Proper 6

(Sunday between June 12 and June 18 inclusive)

COMPLEMENTARY

2 Samuel 11:26–12:10, 13–15   Galatians 2:15–21
Psalm 32   Luke 7:36–8:3

OPENING WORDS / CALL TO WORSHIP
    [Women:] **Come, you who are sinners searching
             for wholeness.**
      [Men:] **Come, you for whom law-keeping is death.**
    [Youth:] **Come, you who cannot save yourselves.**
       [All:] **God who is Three-in-One has done what neither
             the law nor we could do.**
      [Men:] **God the life-giver has kept the law for us;**
    [Women:] **God the self-giver has taken up the
             cross for us;**
    [Youth:] **God the love-giver renews our souls.**
       [All:] **Come; let us worship the triune God.**
[or]
    God is our hiding place, our helper in trouble.   *Ps. 32*
    Our Savior surrounds us in times of distress.
    Be glad in the Lord and rejoice, O righteous!
    Shout for joy, all you upright in heart!

CALL TO CONFESSION
    Happy are those whose sin is forgiven.   *Ps. 32:1–3*
    Keep silence no longer—
    cry out to God, who will answer with mercy.
[or]
    The grace of God is a free gift;   *Gal. 2*
    there is nothing we can do to earn it.
    We receive it through faith,
    by believing in Jesus Christ, our Savior.

Trusting in Christ's mercy,
and with gratitude for this free and precious gift,
let us confess our sin.

PRAYER OF CONFESSION

Gracious God, *Luke 7–8*
you know what kind of people we are.
We judge others harshly
and fail to see our own sin.
We look with suspicion and fear,
and neglect to show hospitality to strangers.
We treasure things that are worthless
and squander your precious gifts.
We withhold the grace and love
that you give us so freely.
Forgive us.
Pour out your grace upon us
to save us from our sin. Amen.

DECLARATION OF FORGIVENESS

I have been crucified with Christ; *Gal. 2*
and it is no longer I who live,
but Christ who lives in me!
The life we now live in the flesh
we live by faith in the Son of God
who loves us and gives himself for us.
Hear the good news!
In Jesus Christ we are forgiven.
Thanks be to God.

PRAYER OF THE DAY

Great God of love, we praise you— *Luke 7–8*
for you wash away the dust of death,
you kiss away the shame of sin,
and anoint us with your Holy Spirit.
Pour out your blessing in this place,
and let your grace flow through our lives
as we spread the news of your saving love;
through Jesus Christ our Lord. Amen.

PRAYER FOR ILLUMINATION

God of steadfast love,   *Ps. 32:8–10*
by the guidance of your Spirit
instruct and teach us
in the way we should go;
through Jesus Christ our Lord. **Amen.**

PRAYERS OF INTERCESSION

To you, O God, we pray—
to you we lift our hearts and voices.   *Ps. 5*

[optional response to each intercession:]
Give ear to our words, O Lord;
listen to our cry.   *Ps. 5:1–2*

For all leaders of nations,
give humility and wisdom.   *2 Sam.12*

For all servants of Christ,
give faith and love.   *Gal. 2*

For all victims of violence,
give justice and peace.   *1 Kgs. 21*

For all captives and debtors,
give freedom and forgiveness.   *Luke 7–8*

For all people who suffer,
give healing and hope.   *Ps. 32*

These things we pray
by your Word and Spirit;
may your will be done. **Amen.**

INVITATION TO THE OFFERING

Christ poured out his life   *Luke 7–8*
in love for the world.
How else can we respond
but with gratitude,
giving our lives in his service?

PRAYER OF THANKSGIVING/DEDICATION

We give you thanks, O God, for the great love *Luke 7–8*
that you have lavished upon us in Christ Jesus.
Teach us to share this love with others,
bringing the good news of your holy realm
to all the ends of the earth;
through Jesus Christ our Lord. **Amen.**

CHARGE

Live to God *Gal. 2:19–20*
and let the love of Christ
live in you.

BLESSING

By the grace of God, *Gal. 2:16; Luke 17:50*
we are saved through faith;
go in peace.

Questions for Reflection

In Luke 7:36–8:3 we hear of a sinful woman who shows great love to Jesus because her sins have been forgiven. Jesus tells a parable about a debtor who shows great love to the one who has canceled his great debt. We regularly pray, "forgive us our debts as we forgive our debtors" or "forgive us our sins as we forgive those who sin against us." How do you show your love to God for the grace you have received in Jesus Christ? How do you show Christ's great love to others?

Household Prayer: Morning

In the morning, O Lord,
we watch and wait for you.
Listen to our voices! Hear our prayer.
Lead us in your righteousness this day
and make your way clear before us;
through Christ Jesus the way. Amen.

Household Prayer: Evening

Lord God,
as the night surrounds us,
be our hiding place
and preserve us from trouble.
Keep your eye upon us
and stay near to us.
Surround us with your steadfast love;
in Jesus' name we pray. Amen.

Proper 7

(Sunday between June 19 and June 25 inclusive)

SEMICONTINUOUS

1 Kings 19:1–4 (5–7), 8–15a   Galatians 3:23–29
Psalm 42 and 43   Luke 8:26–39

OPENING WORDS / CALL TO WORSHIP
When forces in the world threaten us,
when our bodies or spirits turn against us,
there is One who seeks us,
One who meets us,
One who heals us,
whose love washes over us
and sets us free for joy.
This One is the Lord.
Come, let us worship God.

CALL TO CONFESSION
The geography of sin is a waterless waste.
But God gives springs of living water,
streams of justice and mercy splashing
into the wilderness
from the mountain of God.
Let us drink deeply of Christ.
Let us confess our sins.

PRAYER OF CONFESSION
Holy One, God Most High,
grant us faith to confess our sins
and seek your mercy.
There are barren places in our lives
where we have wandered far from you.
We have listened to voices
who distracted us from your call.

We have submitted to powers
competing for our loyalty to you.
We have not taken the hand you offer
to lead us out of godforsakenness,
and into your holy ways.
God our Savior, forgive us.
Quench our thirst for you
from the Rock of our salvation,
and let your love well up in us
unto eternal life.
Speak tenderly to us of your presence.
Feed us with your word.
Deliver us from evil.
Let us enter into your kingdom;
then send us out to serve you
by the power of the Holy Spirit,
in the name of your Son, Jesus Christ. Amen.

DECLARATION OF FORGIVENESS

Christ Jesus is the bread of life,   *John 6:35, 48–52;*
manna come down from heaven.   *Col. 3:3*
Christ covers us with baptismal waters,
so that our lives are hidden in him.
This Jesus, the Son of the Most High God,
is sovereign even over the powers of evil,
so that his reign brings freedom and joy.
Therefore, I declare to you
by the power of the Holy Spirit,
in Jesus Christ our sins are forgiven. **Amen.**

PRAYER OF THE DAY

Almighty God,
ruler of all things seen and unseen,
through your Son, Jesus Christ
and the Holy Spirit,
you show your power and mercy.
You cast out evil,
tear down walls of division,
comfort and challenge your people,
and show signs of your kingdom

coming into the world.
Grant that we
may lift up the discouraged,
strengthen the doubting,
and join with all who seek
to thank you for your goodness.
Glory be to you, O God,
who, with the Holy Spirit and the Holy Son,
together is worshiped and praised;
One God forever. **Amen.**

PRAYER FOR ILLUMINATION

Holy, Holy, Holy One,
your words feed us,
the Word frees us,
and the Spirit gives us life.
Grant our ears an appetite for hearing
and our spirits strength for loving you. **Amen.**

PRAYERS OF INTERCESSION

Holy God of earth and sky,
in your presence mountains quake,
flames tremble,
and the winds roar
"Hallelujah!"

We pray for the coming of your kingdom.
Let the earth be made whole and new;
let the sky be made clean and refreshed.
May all who dwell in heaven
and throughout the world
be joined in giving you praise.

We pray for the nations
and people of the world.
Let us receive your reign with gladness.
Grant world leaders wisdom and humility,
that they may guide your flocks
in the ways that make for peace.
Give us ears to attend to the voices

of poets and prophets,
through whom your Spirit speaks.

We pray for the most vulnerable:
for creatures threatened with extinction . . .
for those of the human family
who are poor, homeless, or refugees . . .
victims of political or domestic violence . . .
those who are ill in body, mind, or spirit . . . .
Grant us compassionate hearts,
inspired minds,
and wills resolved
to care for our neighbors
with the love of Christ Jesus.

When you bring your promised kingdom,
all your creatures will shout, "Glory!"
all your people will sigh, "Love,"
and all creation will together sing,
"Hallelujah!" **Amen.**

INVITATION TO THE OFFERING
God gives us more than enough
for our journey of faith.
Let us present our tithes and offerings
so that others may know their blessings
and give thanks to God.

PRAYER OF THANKSGIVING/DEDICATION
Triune God,
through Jesus Christ
and the power of the Holy Spirit,
you bring hope to the despairing,
healing to the sick,
and release from bondage
to all who are oppressed by sin and evil.
Through baptism into Christ,
you cover us with your love.
We thank you
that in that flood you wash away

all that separates us from you
and one another.
We thank you that in this new life
we are set free
to proclaim good news to others.
Direct our gifts to fulfill your purpose
as we await the time
when all creation is one in your love,
by the grace of Jesus Christ
and the community of the Holy Spirit. **Amen.**

CHARGE

Worship God alone—
God of the prophets,
Jesus Christ, the Son of God,
and the Spirit of the Holy One.
Do not be overcome by evil powers.
Trust God,
who even the powers must obey.
Rejoice in your salvation,
by loving others,
to the glory of God,
who is Three, who is One.

BLESSING

God feed you;
Christ protect you;
Spirit live in you
and wash over you
with the love of God.

Questions for Reflection

When do I feel the most separated from God? When do I feel closest
to God?

Household Prayer: Morning

Dear God,
today I will be tempted

to wander away from you.
By your Spirit, guide me
in the ways you want me to go.
I may become discouraged
by my own limitations
or by interactions I have with others.
Direct my thoughts and words and actions
so that they reflect your love,
not only for me,
but also for those around me.
Remind me
today and every day
that, in Jesus Christ,
I belong to you.
That will be enough. Amen.

Household Prayer: Evening

Creator of day and night,
as shadows lengthen
let me gather my thoughts
and feelings before you.
Thank you for your presence today.
Watch over me through the night.
Be with those who are wakeful,
either because they are doing their work,
caring for others,
or because of trouble
that will not let them rest.
Grant to all your peace,
and the promise that your kingdom is coming
as surely as the morning light.
In this hope let all your people trust,
giving you thanks and praise
tonight, tomorrow, and forever. Amen.

Proper 7

(Sunday between June 19 and June 25 inclusive)

COMPLEMENTARY

Isaiah 65:1–9	Galatians 3:23–29
Psalm 22:19–28	Luke 8:26–39

OPENING WORDS / CALL TO WORSHIP
There is no longer Jew or Greek,   *Gal. 3:26, 28*
there is no longer slave or free,
there is no longer male and female:
for all of you are one in Christ Jesus.
We are children of God through faith.

CALL TO CONFESSION
Trusting in the mercy of God,
let us confess our sin to God and to one another.

PRAYER OF CONFESSION
Merciful and gracious God,
we walk in a way that is not good.
We follow our own devices.
We ignore your image in ourselves and in our neighbors.
Do not turn away from us, O God,
but hear our cry for blessing.
Lead us out of the tombs we inhabit.
Guide us into your light
so that we may walk in your way. Amen.

DECLARATION OF FORGIVENESS
You belong to Christ and are heirs of the promise of freedom.
In full assurance of justification by grace through faith,
by the authority of God's beloved Son,
I declare to you the absolute forgiveness of all your sins.
In the name of the blessed Trinity, One God. **Amen.**

PRAYER OF THE DAY

Living God,
you call us to yourself
so that we may live in wholeness
with ourselves and our neighbors.
Unchain your people
and set us free to rejoice in your saving word,
through Jesus Christ, our Savior. **Amen.**

PRAYER FOR ILLUMINATION

As you spoke to the Legions, O God,
speak now to the forces that surround us.
By your Spirit, let your word illumine the darkness,
and your light break through our delusions,
that we may see your truth. **Amen.**

PRAYERS OF INTERCESSION

We pray now for all the world,
the church, people of faith,
and those who live in want, saying:
God, in your mercy, hear our prayer.

God of kings, prophets, children, and all
    who are in need,
we give you thanks for the breath of life
you pour into the living
and into us all when we are in trouble.
Bless your world in times of struggle and days
    of rejoicing.
Make us one with you and one another.
God, in your mercy, **hear our prayer.**

We thank you for your care of the earth,
especially for rain and sun,
for the flowers that give food to bees,
for fish in all their shapes and colors,
and for the shelter we find underneath your trees.
Let all creation praise your name.
God, in your mercy, **hear our prayer.**

We pray for the church,
that fellowship in this congregation,
and in the families of faith in all the lands,
give us both comfort and challenge.
Teach us to give thanks for insights new to us.
Make us able to rejoice with people of other faiths
that Christians, Jews, Buddhists, Hindus, Muslims,
    and others
may speak kindly of one another.
God, in your mercy, **hear our prayer.**

We pray for people everywhere to take courage,
especially this day the people of [*name nations in turmoil or
    need at the present time*].
who face uncertain futures.
God, in your mercy, **hear our prayer.**

For widows, widowers, divorced parents,
children, orphans, all who live alone,
families of origin, and families formed by friendship,
that they find love in community and comfort in you.
God, in your mercy, **hear our prayer.**

For all in any need:
for those enduring cancer treatments,
those awaiting and recovering from surgery,
those reshaping their lives from tornadoes, fires, and floods;
for people who have no food, no work, no self-respect,
and for those we name now aloud or in our hearts . . . *[silence]*.
God, in your mercy, **hear our prayer.**

For all the saints who from their labors now rest, especially *N*.
God, in your mercy, **hear our prayer.**

We place into your safekeeping all for whom we pray,
trusting that in your wisdom,
the needs of all people will be met,
through Jesus Christ our Lord. **Amen.**

INVITATION TO THE OFFERING

For the sake of those who have yet to hear the word of God,
for those who are in need of our bounty,
and for the discipline that comes with sacrifice,
let us bring our tithes and offerings.

PRAYER OF THANKSGIVING/DEDICATION

With these gifts, O God,
we remember with thanksgiving
the life that we have because of you.
Make us grateful every day
for the privilege of offering ourselves
for the well-being of all your world. **Amen.**

[or]

Thanks be to you, Creator of the universe,
for earth and sky,
water and rock,
creatures and plants,
that we may have life enough to live and to offer for others.

Thanks be to you, Crucified and Risen Lord,
who shows us the face of God
so that we may see in our brothers and sisters
a member of Christ's own body and rejoice.

Thanks be to you, Holy Spirit, Giver of Life,
who groans within us as we pray
and teaches us compassion
that we might love our neighbors as ourselves.

Accept our offerings as signs of your never-failing care,
in the name of all that is most precious in your sight. **Amen.**

CHARGE

Go in peace to care for those who cross your path,
to give voice to those who need your help,
to notice what is beautiful and what is amiss,
to counter injustice and guard what is good, and
to rest and work, mindful of God's desire
for your health and faith.

BLESSING

The Lord bless you and keep you.
The Lord's face shine on you with grace and mercy.
The Lord look upon you with favor and give you peace.

Questions for Reflection

Think of the many ways in which people are "chained" and how the word of God speaks differently to those prisons. What specific constraint is in your own life for which you might pray that the Holy Spirit show you a path toward freedom?

Household Prayer: Morning

Gracious and loving God,
we give you thanks for protection through the night
and for your presence throughout the day.
Clothe us with mercy toward those we meet.
Render us the courage and calm we need
to face the tasks of the present
and to prepare for the challenges to come.
Guard us this day so that we learn
to give thanks at all times.
In Jesus' name we pray. Amen.

Household Prayer: Evening

Almighty and gracious God,
we give you thanks for this day of work and play,
for study and chores,
for time with our family and friends,
and for time to be alone.
Bring us now to the peace of mind that lets us rest in you.
Refresh us with your care
so that we may rise in the morning with joy. Amen.

Proper 8

(Sunday between June 26 and July 2 inclusive)

SEMICONTINUOUS

2 Kings 2:1–2, 6–14   Galatians 5:1, 13–25
Psalm 77:1–2, 11–20   Luke 9:51–62

OPENING WORDS / CALL TO WORSHIP
God, who rules the universe, calls us;
Christ, who took up his cross, calls us;
Holy Spirit, who frees us body and soul, calls us.
Let us faithfully answer
by worshiping the triune God.

CALL TO CONFESSION
Christ Jesus did not call down destruction   *Luke 9:52–55*
upon those who rejected him.
How much more will he show mercy
to those who seek forgiveness.
In faith, let us confess our sins.

PRAYER OF CONFESSION
O God, Holy Trinity,
help us to confess our sins.
You give us a place in your creation,
and you intend that we live in love
with all that you have made.
We confess that we abuse what you give us.
By our thoughts, actions,
and the meditations of our hearts
we show how enslaved we are
to life made corrupt by sin.
Far from walking in the Spirit,
we stumble on paths that lead to death.

O Fire of heaven,
have mercy on us.
Satisfy the longings of our souls
by taking us up into your Spirit
that we may love our neighbor.
Rekindle our desire
to follow our Savior, Jesus Christ,
whose passion for obeying you
leads us to our inheritance,
which is your promised kingdom.
To you and the Son and the Spirit,
One God,
be all worship and praise
now and forever. Amen.

DECLARATION OF FORGIVENESS

The crucified Christ has set us free
to live in the Spirit of life.
Hear the good news of the gospel.
In Jesus Christ, we are forgiven.

PRAYER OF THE DAY

As prophets catch fire,
as disciples draw flame,
as apostles walk in the Spirit,
O Holy One, Holy Three,
fill us with fervent desire
to enter your kingdom.
Lead us by the cross of Christ
to live in the love of Christ,
now and forever. **Amen.**

PRAYER FOR ILLUMINATION

O God,
by your Spirit plant your word within us
that we may follow your Son,
our Lord, Jesus Christ,
and never leave him.
May we find our home

in your kingdom
and our life in your Spirit. **Amen.**

[A time of silence is kept after each intercession.]
God of the angels and the saints in light,
head of the church catholic and apostolic,
midwife of the new creation,
hear us as we pray
for the coming of your kingdom. . . . *[silent prayer]*
Cleanse the pollution of the world
caused by human sin.
Receive the body of the earth,
and the bodies of your children
into your holy presence.
Dwell with us and be our light.

Hear us as we pray
for the healing of the nations. . . . *[silent prayer]*
Silence the wars and rumors of terror
that plague the human family.
Guide leaders of the world
to the river and the tree of life.
May the fruits of the Spirit
feed the people of the earth.

Hear us as we pray for all who suffer. . . . *[silent prayer]*
Lift the yoke of human pain
from the sick, especially *N.,*
the hungry,
and the grieving, especially *N.*
Move the hearts of your people
to serve all who are in need.

Hear us as we pray
for the Church. . . . *[silent prayer]*
Lay the mantle of Elijah
on the shoulders of the people of God.
Let the Spirit shine in the eyes
of the body of Christ.

With a mighty voice,
let the church roar, "Justice!"
With a tender kiss,
let her pray, "Mercy."
With the sign of the cross,
let her say,
"Peace be with you,"
in the name of the Lord Jesus Christ. **Amen.**

INVITATION TO THE OFFERING

The blessings that come from God
are rich like the fruits of summer.
With our tithes and our offerings
let us give thanks and praise to the triune God:
to the Son for our salvation,
the Spirit for our rising,
and the Creator of heaven and earth.

PRAYER OF THANKSGIVING/DEDICATION

God our maker, our Savior, our source of life,
we thank you for your self-giving love.
You made us in your image
and gave us a home in your world.
You did not forsake us
when our sin brought disaster
upon what you love.
Instead, you sojourned with us
in the wasteland;
you taught us neighbor-love and holiness
through the commands of Moses;
you spoke to us
words of justice, correction, and kindness
in the poetry of the prophets.
We thank you
that in the fullness of time
you sent the Son
to be born of Mary by the Holy Spirit,
to be the perfect image of God.
We thank you
that Christ Jesus gave himself upon the cross

to free us from the bondage to sin and death.
We thank you
for receiving him in resurrection and ascension,
the firstborn of the new creation.
Through him we have freedom
to walk in the Spirit that is eternal life.
We present our offerings and commit ourselves
to follow Jesus Christ,
love our neighbors,
and share the fruits of the Spirit,
giving you thanks and praise,
O holy, triune God. **Amen.**

CHARGE

Let your life show the goodness of God.
Pray with your body.
Thank the Spirit for simple pleasures.
Guard your mind and spirit
against false desires or ambitions
that would lead you away
from loving your neighbor as yourself.
Build up the community around you;
live at peace in the body of Christ.
Be loyal to that which is worthy
of your loyalty:
God's presence and God's future.

BLESSING

God makes you free
as an eagle riding the wind.
Christ gives you a home
in the kingdom he is bringing.
The Holy Spirit fills your belly with fire,
and your heart with joy.

Questions for Reflection

To what is God calling me? How might others know that I walk in the
Spirit with Christ?

Household Prayer: Morning

Almighty God,
in awe I remember that you made me in your image
and breathed the Spirit of life into me.
I marvel that your Son, Jesus,
took on flesh and bone just like mine,
and gave himself for my salvation.
Help me to live this day
fully open to your presence.
Let me worship you alone
with my body, mind, and spirit,
delighting in what is good
and turning from what is not.
Let me love my neighbor as myself
with all that you give me.
Be patient with me,
and help me to be patient with others.
Teach me how to bring peace
to those who are troubled
and to show kindness,
especially to the weak.
Today, let me seek your kingdom,
through Jesus Christ, my Lord. Amen.

Household Prayer: Evening

O God, guardian of your people,
thank you for your care today.
As I move into evening,
help me to recall with thanksgiving
the wonders I have known,
the joy I have felt,
and your love I have received.
Forgive me
for the ways in which I misused
what you intend for good.
Jesus had nowhere to rest his head;
let me rest in him.

I pray for all who are dear to me,
that they, too, may abide in your care.
Grant the peace of sleep
to all who are weary;
and let us rise to a new day,
giving you praise
as we prepare for the eternal day
you are bringing
through Jesus Christ, the Lord,
to whom, with you and the Holy Spirit,
be all honor and glory,
now and forever. Amen.

Proper 8

(Sunday between June 26 and July 2 inclusive)

COMPLEMENTARY

1 Kings 19:15–16, 19–21   Galatians 5:1, 13–25
Psalm 16   Luke 9:51–62

OPENING WORDS / CALL TO WORSHIP
Jesus calls to the crowds with warnings.
Jesus calls to the converts to follow him.
Jesus calls to the resisters with parables of rejection.
Jesus calls to you: "Proclaim the kingdom of God."
And the people answer:
Thanks be to God
for life and health and all goodness.

CALL TO CONFESSION
Clothed with the mantle of baptism
and protected by God's promise of forgiveness,
let us confess our sins to God and to one another.

PRAYER OF CONFESSION
Merciful God,
we confess that we desire what is not your will.
We fear failure
and cling to unquestioned habits.
We are truly sorry and repent
of what we have done
and what we have not done.
Show us the path of your prophetic way.
Open our eyes to new ventures.
Help us love our neighbors as ourselves.
Forgive us and renew us,
in the name of life abundant,
Jesus Christ our Lord. Amen.

DECLARATION OF FORGIVENESS

The fruits of the spirit are love, joy, and peace
given to you through God's grace.
By the power vested in me
as a minister of the church of Jesus Christ,
I proclaim that you are forgiven.
Live in the word of the Lord and be made new.

PRAYER OF THE DAY

Holy and gracious God,
you call us to ventures that cannot be foretold,
to paths we do not know.
Be our guide, through your word,
and feed us with your assurance
that your way is truly the path of love, joy, and peace. **Amen.**

PRAYER FOR ILLUMINATION

Your word, O God,
reveals your will for our lives.
By the power of your Holy Spirit,
give us each the wisdom to attend to your call every day,
and make us ready to hear and obey.
Through Jesus Christ our Lord. **Amen.**

PRAYERS OF INTERCESSION

We pray now in Jesus' name for the church, the world,
and all who are in need, saying,
    Hear us, O God; your mercy is great.

Holy God of healing and peace,
we thank you for life and health;
for morning and evening;
for rain and sun;
for all you give us to sustain life;
and most of all for Jesus,
who died and rose again to make real the promise of new life.
    Hear us, O God; **your mercy is great.**

We ask, O God, for a church that ministers every day
to bring people together in your name,

for hearts that will not judge,
for minds that recognize injustice and oppression in all
    its forms,
for hands that are open to answer your call.
    Hear us, O God; **your mercy is great.**

Merciful God, the nations you have called into being
are many and full of marvels.
We pray for their well-being;
for leaders and workers;
teachers and soldiers;
scholars, artists, parents, and peacemakers;
for nations and peoples in strife, especially for *N.*;
that your way be known in all the lands and joy may reign.
    Hear us, O God; **your mercy is great.**

Turn our hearts, Holy One,
to respect and honor those who are not like us;
let us see in peoples of every nation
the majesty of your desire for richness and difference.
    Hear us, O God; **your mercy is great.**

We pray for bodies and spirits healed,
for those who are in pain,
for those awaiting surgery,
for those who are struggling with physical therapies,
for those awaiting death,
and for those we name now aloud or silently . . . *[silence]*
    Hear us, O God; **your mercy is great.**

We ask your special blessing, O God,
on the children in our communities,
for their play and work in this summertime
to give them strength and renewal;
for an ever-increasing opening of their minds,
new ways of seeing,
new understandings of the gifts you call them to use;
and for their happiness and health.
    Hear us, O God; **your mercy is great.**

For the secret burdens we lift before you now,
either silently or aloud . . . *[silence]*
>Hear us, O God; **your mercy is great.**

We give you thanks for the saints
who have taught us how to listen to your word,
how to answer your desire for our lives,
and how to teach and proclaim your love to others.
>Hear us, O God; **your mercy is great.**

Into your hands we place our prayers
and all whose welfare we entrust to your care.
Bless them and all who have needs only you can know.
In thanksgiving for all your gifts,
we pray this in the name of the one God, Mother of us all. **Amen.**

INVITATION TO THE OFFERING
As Jesus set his face toward Jerusalem
to offer himself for the sake of the world,
let us now offer our tithes and gifts in thanksgiving.

PRAYER OF THANKSGIVING/DEDICATION
Take these gifts, O God, for the work of this church.
Let them stand as signs of your love and faithfulness.
In the name of the one who gave himself for us, we pray. **Amen.**
[or]
Gracious God,
you give us your creation for our home
and fill it with the necessities of life.
You give us yourself as Jesus,
our teacher, friend, and savior
whose life, death, resurrection, and ascension
show us daily your love for your people.
You give us your Holy Spirit,
who fills our hearts with prayer
and by whose light we hear your word.
Bless these gifts,
and make us truly thankful.
All glory and honor is yours,
now and forever. **Amen.**

CHARGE

Live in hope, love with mercy, leave no stone unturned
in your calling as one of God's precious disciples.
For as often as you heed the word of the Lord,
you are turned toward what is good and beautiful.

BLESSING

May the holy Trinity, one God,
bless you and keep you,
now and forever.

Questions for Reflection

What new mantle is God placing on your shoulders? Where in your life is
the new beginning, the unfamiliar task, the calling to a path on which the
ending is yet unclear?

Household Prayer: Morning

God of renewal and joy,
thank you for a night of rest, for home, for companionship,
and for all the gifts of Earth that make our lives possible.
Give us this day the sustenance needed
for the work we have ahead of us.
Keep our vision clear and our resolve strong.
Bless us, in Jesus' name. Amen.

Household Prayer: Evening

For this day, O God, we give you thanks.
In all the joys that came our way,
the challenges that showed us more about your world,
the people who made our meals and journeys,
you revealed your care.
Keep us now this night from harm
that when we rise from sleep,
we will again give thanks and praise to you.
Bless us, in Jesus' name. Amen.

Proper 9

(Sunday between July 3 and July 9 inclusive)

SEMICONTINUOUS

2 Kings 5:1–14	Galatians 6:(1–6) 7–16
Psalm 30	Luke 10:1–11, 16–20

OPENING WORDS / CALL TO WORSHIP
Call upon the Lord!
I asked for help and I was healed!
We asked for freedom,
and we were given liberty beyond measure!
Praise God!

Sing to the Lord, all you faithful;
give thanks to God's holy name.
God turned our mourning into dancing!
The Great Tailor took away the sackcloth
and dressed us up in celebration!
Our hearts sing without ceasing!
O Lord our God, we will always give you thanks!

CALL TO CONFESSION
When we walk from darkness into the light
we can see ourselves as we really are.
We see the spots of sin more clearly,
and we realize that we need God's healing and redemption.
Come and confess your sins to God,
and wade into the river of the Healer's mercy.

PRAYER OF CONFESSION
God, you have caught us in our sinful behavior.
We come to you with the hope of your restoration.
We walk with our heads held high,
without noticing others and their burdens.

70

We are even blinded to our own!
We keep our mouths silenced
when we are full of stories to share
about the good things that you have done for us.
We even keep our actions silenced
as we become so overwhelmed with the needs of the world
that we do nothing to overcome them.

Fill us with your peace and with your mercy.
Free us from the destruction of sin
and restore us to a life
lived in you. Amen.

DECLARATION OF FORGIVENESS

Peace!
Peace is what you receive from God
when you know that your sins are forgiven.
Peace is what you have when you know
that the destruction of sin cannot harm you,
because you are not alone in your journey of life.
Therefore, peace, my sisters and brothers!
In Jesus we have received forgiveness,
and we have been restored!
Thanks be to God!

PRAYER OF THE DAY

O God, you send us out into the world
as your disciples.
Allow the church to be a healing presence,
a place and a people that live out the essence
of your kingdom, here and now;
through Jesus Christ our Lord,
who lives and reigns with you and the Holy Spirit,
one God, forever. **Amen.**

PRAYER FOR ILLUMINATION

Your Word, O Lord,
is our inspiration, our light, and our motion.
Your Word, O Lord,
is power, is wisdom, and is comfort.

Guide us today, as we listen to the Word
read and proclaimed,
and fill us with understanding
and with the desire to change.
Speak Lord! Your people listen! **Amen.**

PRAYERS OF INTERCESSION
Let us pray for the needs of the world, saying,
Lord of mercy, lift us out of the depths!
[The leader may gesture to the assembly to indicate their response.]

God of prophets and of disciples,
you have heard the plea of your people
throughout the ages.
Hear us now,
as we present to you
those things that burden us.
Lord of mercy,
lift us out of the depths!

Hear us as we pray for those who are sick.
Give them hope,
that they may feel through your presence,
and the presence of others,
comfort and support.
Grant them patience,
that they may live
in your time
and in your will.
We believe
in the power of your healing!
Do your will, God. Do your will!
Lord of mercy,
lift us out of the depths!

Hear us as we pray for those who live in constant conflict.
Bring your wisdom to their lives.
Enable your people to learn from you,
whose anger lasts only a moment,
but whose favor lasts a lifetime.

Allow our anger to last only a moment,
that we might put our efforts
toward reconciliation and peace.
Lord of mercy,
lift us out of the depths!

Hear us as we pray for those who feel
imprisoned by temptation and sin.
Lead us to examine ourselves and our lives
to see how and why
we fall into temptation,
and give us empathy to understand others and
    their prisons.
Grant us the strength to do good and to not
    be weary,
and to always be watchful for opportunities to
    do your will.
Lord of mercy,
lift us out of the depths!

Holy God, we pray for your church.
Give us courage to be true disciples.
The world outside these walls can be challenging,
and yet others watch us
as we witness and we act.
Give us wisdom to better reflect
your actions of love and mercy,
so that our families, our communities,
and our countries
might understand
what your kingdom is all about.
We pray in the name of your perfect witness in the world,
Jesus Christ, our Lord and Savior. **Amen.**

INVITATION TO THE OFFERING

God has given us healing, word, forgiveness.
God has given us so much!
Let us now take the time
to respond in gratitude,
by giving of what has been given to us.

PRAYER OF THANKSGIVING/DEDICATION

Let us give thanks to the Lord our God!
It is right to give thanks and praise!

Your church exalts you!
In your mercy,
you have given us life everlasting,
you have given us freedom from death,
and you have favored us.
In your love,
you have given us the strength
to stand up and continue on our journey.
In your wisdom,
you have taken a chance on us,
by allowing us to be part
of your holy plans and your message.

Help us to use the gifts
you have given us
with mercy, love, and wisdom,
so that we can continue to honor
the trust you have put on us.
In the name of Jesus Christ we pray. **Amen.**

CHARGE

The harvest truly is great.
There is a need for peace in the world.
The harvest truly is great.
People are sick and in need of solace.
The harvest truly is great.
Humanity needs to hear that the kingdom of God has come.
God calls us to go and labor in the harvest.
Don't hesitate! Don't be weary!
Jesus has promised that he will give us
the power needed to do God's will.
Let us go rejoicing!

BLESSING

May the God who heals
accompany you with hope

so that you may face life's uncertainties.
May the teacher, Jesus Christ,
send you out as disciples
certain of his words and power.
And may the Holy Spirit fill you with an unceasing desire
to do good wherever you are.
Blessed are the ones who go in the name of the Lord!

Questions for Reflection

God heals and commands us to go out into the world and heal others.
How are you a healing person? What situations around you are in need of
healing? How can the church be an agent of healing?

Household Prayer: Morning

Each morning when we wake up
we are reminded of your presence.
The light of the sun, the sounds of the birds, . . .
your creation serves as witness
of your love and your imagination.
Let us take it all in
and transform our awe into praises
that those around us
can hear each day
and know that you are God. Amen.

Household Prayer: Evening

We have heard your voice, O God.
Through smiles, through words,
through music, through tears, . . .
we have heard your voice!
Give us the comfort of your presence
as we begin to live out the end of our day,
and allow us to have rest
and the same peace that your disciples declared
when they entered somebody's home and said,
"Peace to this house." Amen.

Proper 9

(Sunday between July 3 and July 9 inclusive)

COMPLEMENTARY

Isaiah 66:10–14	Galatians 6:(1–6) 7–16
Psalm 66:1–9	Luke 10:1–11, 16–20

OPENING WORDS / CALL TO WORSHIP

Sing praise to the Lord, all you faithful: *Ps. 30:4*
give thanks in holy remembrance.

CALL TO CONFESSION

Secure in the promise of God's knowledge of us,
and trusting in God's readiness to forgive,
let us confess our sin.

PRAYER OF CONFESSION

Source of all that gives us life,
we have turned away from your authority
to our own small concerns.
Forgive us for our failure to bear one another's
    burdens,
for boasting of anything but your cross,
for believing in our own power to justify
    our lives,
and for denying your call to take comfort in
    you alone.
Lead us to the river of life
that in all we do, we may honor your name. Amen.

DECLARATION OF FORGIVENESS

In the name of the one who died and rose for us,
and by the authority of the church's ordination,
I declare to you full forgiveness of your sins
for new life.

PRAYER OF THE DAY

Holy God, you are for all the world
a river of shelter and nourishment,
a city of joy and riches,
the defender of those you love.
Take us into your arms again this day
and feed us with the power of your comfort;
through Jesus Christ, our Savior. **Amen.**

PRAYER FOR ILLUMINATION

Bring us to the bosom of your Word, O God,
and feed us on your truth,
that we may have the strength you have promised
    your children. **Amen.**

PRAYERS OF INTERCESSION

Let us pray for the needs of the world, saying,
    Gracious God, hear our prayer.

God, our Mother and Father,
we give you thanks that you have brought us to this new day.
The beauty and power of sunshine,
wind, fog, and rain are marvels to our senses,
and in them we see how much we depend on your gifts.
Even in the darkest storms,
help us to see in nature's might
the guiding hand in which you hold your children.
    Gracious God, **hear our prayer.**

Pour out on us a spirit of grace and petition,
as on Jerusalem of old,
and hear us in our need:
that the law of faith which guides us
be our standard in judging the laws of land and church and culture,
and that our lives be conformed to the faithful love of Christ.
    Gracious God, **hear our prayer.**

That we who call Christ "Messiah"
be empowered to carry the cross of insult
as we work for freedom;

that all nations may be steered by leaders
who value each individual in their care;
that all people may work for the good of everyone.
    Gracious God, **hear our prayer.**

That the paths we walk be wide enough for all people:
for the homeless,
for aliens in flight,
for prisoners,
for persons of all colors,
for all who are ostracized,
for those dying of incurable disease,
for all who you call your own.
    Gracious God, **hear our prayer.**

That children may grow up strong and kind;
that we give thanks to you for new life;
that families be strengthened for the sake of each member.
    Gracious God, **hear our prayer.**

That all people weakened through illness of mind or body
feel your protective hand and our tangible care;
that healing of body and soul come to N.
Give to your people all that you see is needed.
    Gracious God, **hear our prayer.**

That all who mourn will know the consolation of your love,
and that you bless all we name now in our hearts and aloud . . . .
    [silence]
    Gracious God, **hear our prayer.**

With unending gratitude,
we remember our ancestors,
your children,
the saints of the church whose lives
continue to witness to your power.
We especially remember N. this day.
    Gracious God, **hear our prayer.**

Into your hands we entrust all for whom we pray,
assured that you hear us and send us your aid;
through Jesus Christ our Lord. **Amen.**

INVITATION TO THE OFFERING

Let us not grow weary in doing what is right,
for the Lord has given us all that we have,
and in gratitude, we respond with our offerings.

PRAYER OF THANKSGIVING/DEDICATION

In you, O God, we take refuge.
You are the source of all our hope,
the font of all wisdom.
You created the world and feed it daily.
You cradle your people in safety.
You call your creatures everywhere
to grow and live according to your purposes.
You sent us your Son
to give life and vision.
You guard us with your Holy Spirit
even in the midst of those who would destroy
what you have made.
Let these gifts be signs of your creative hand
in the places where there is need.
Bless the work of your people.
We ask this in the name of the one
who knows us through and through—
Jesus Christ, our Lord and Savior. **Amen.**

CHARGE

Lean on the nourishment of the Lord,
that it may feed you to work for the good of all.
Let the cross be your boasting and your pride
and the people of God your family.
Reaping what we sow,
bearing one another's burdens,
let the harvest be pleasing
in the sight of God.

BLESSING

Now may the crucified and risen Lord,
who cradles you and nourishes all the earth,
keep you from every weariness,
and raise you up to live
in the comfort of the reign of God.

Questions for Reflection

Responding to the boasting of the disciples he sent out, Jesus said,
"I watched Satan fall from heaven like a flash of lightning" (Luke 10:18).
What does Jesus' response indicate? What is he saying? Where and when
have you seen Satan fall like lightning?

Household Prayer: Morning

The earth is full of your call to feasting, Holy God,
and you have given us rest for this new day.
Guide us so that in all we do
we may rejoice in the security of your promises.
Make us honest about ourselves and others,
and teach us to move with kindness as we work and play;
in Jesus' name. Amen.

Household Prayer: Evening

As the sky grows dark, O God,
we give you thanks for this day of work and rest,
of fellowship with our family and friends,
of living with the strengths and weaknesses of our bodies.
Give us now the quiet and peace
that will nourish us for tomorrow when, again,
we will look to the Light of the world for hope and joy.
We pray this in Jesus' name. Amen.

Proper 10

(Sunday between July 10 and July 16 inclusive)

SEMICONTINUOUS

Amos 7:7–17   Colossians 1:1–14
Psalm 82   Luke 10:25–37

OPENING WORDS / CALL TO WORSHIP

Love the Lord your God,   *Luke 10:27–28*
with all your heart, and with all your soul,
and with all your strength, and with all your mind!
Love your neighbor as yourself,
with all your heart, and with all your soul,
and with all your strength, and with all your mind!
Do this and you will live!
Let us worship God!

CALL TO CONFESSION

The psalmist asks a question: *Ps. 82:2*
how long?
How long will we live unjustly
and show partiality,
instead of loving as God has loved us?
Trusting in that love,
let us confess our transgressions to the Lord.

PRAYER OF CONFESSION

Holy God,   *Ps. 82*
we are your sons and daughters,
descendants of the God most high,
yet, we do not behave to honor you
and our actions belittle the love you have for us.
We do not defend the weak
or those without fathers or mothers.
We do not uphold the poor or the oppressed.

We do not commit to efforts to rescue
the weak and the needy;
we sometimes deliver them
into solitude and neglect.

Rise up to judge us, O God.
We prefer your merciful justice,
than living with guilt and fear.
Straighten our path,
so that we can be guided
as a mother or a father guides beloved children. Amen.

DECLARATION OF FORGIVENESS

The triune God's unconditional love
does not seek appearances or conditions,
but loves in such a way,
that we are restored to health and to wholeness.
Thanks be to God!
In Jesus Christ,
we are forgiven.
Thanks be to God!

PRAYER OF THE DAY

Holy God,
you call us to live out
your justice and righteousness.
Help us to walk in your footsteps,
so that we never lose our way.
Enable us to live and love
in the way that you have taught us,
so that we can act in grace,
even with those who we consider our enemies.
In the name of Jesus we pray. **Amen.**

PRAYER FOR ILLUMINATION

Holy God, this is the time
when we quiet our hearts and our minds,
to pay attention—
to *really* pay attention—

to what you have to say to us today.
Fill us with your Word,
and give us understanding
by your Holy Spirit,
that having heard your Word,
we may live lives worthy
of you and please you in every way. **Amen.**

PRAYERS OF INTERCESSION
Holy God, your people come
to pray for the world and all that is in it.

God of justice,
work your will in our world.
Free us, O God, to speak your word
in a world that needs to listen to you.
Greed has overtaken the land
and ambition has taken the place of the values
you expect from us.
Iniquity has taken hold,
making the rich richer and the poor poorer.
Give us your voice,
that your church can serve as shepherd,
guiding your people to your will for the world.

God of compassion,
work your will in our world.
Free us, O God, to tend to those
who are weak and needy.
You always care especially
for those abandoned or rejected;
for the sick, women, children, widows.
Give us eyes to recognize them in our midst:
people living with HIV/AIDS;
people without legal immigration documents;
people in abusive relationships;
those who live in the shadows of fear and indifference;
use us to deliver them, with your guiding help,
from all that would harm or oppress.

God of impartiality,
work your will in our world.
Free us, O God, from asking, "Who is our neighbor?"
Take pity on us, that we might show compassion;
anoint us and bandage our wounds,
that we might do the same for those in need.
Carry us,
and give us strength to carry others.

Heal your aching world, we pray,
and use us to work out your will.
In the name of the Father, the Son, and the Holy Spirit. Amen.

INVITATION TO THE OFFERING
As a redeemed people,
we live for giving thanks!
We understand that everything we do
and everything we have,
comes from God, whose unconditional love
lift us up each day.
Let us continue our thanksgiving,
with grateful hearts,
by giving of what God has provided.

PRAYER OF THANKSGIVING/DEDICATION
Thank you God:
you are our soil, our food,
our water, our sun,
everything we need to grow.
We offer these gifts to you,
asking for your direction,
as we work each day
so that your kingdom of light
becomes more and more of a reality
in this world. **Amen.**

CHARGE
Go and bear fruit!
Go and do!
Live a life that is worthy of the Lord.

Give joyful thanks to God
through loving your neighbor,
through doing justice,
through speaking out,
and through defending those
who are weak and oppressed.

BLESSING

May God fill you
with the knowledge of God's will.
May Jesus Christ, who has rescued you,
give you constant faith
to speak the true word of the gospel.
And may the Holy Spirit
guide you in wisdom and understanding,
so that the world can flower with the love of God.

Questions for Reflection

How can we bear God's fruit in the world? How can we live out the
commandment to love God and to love our neighbor as ourselves?

Household Prayer: Morning

Prepare my mind
to listen to you today.
Prepare my heart
to be filled with your love today.
Prepare my lips,
that they can shout your praise today.
Prepare my soul,
that I can be attuned to your will today.
Prepare me to feel your presence
in the world today! Amen.

Household Prayer: Evening

We come together,
and this we pray:
let us love the Lord our God,

with all our hearts,
with all our souls,
with all our strength,
with all our minds,
and let us love our neighbor
as ourselves.
By doing this, O God,
we will truly live,
because we will live
under the guidance of your words,
and the rest that your love provides.
In Jesus' name we pray. Amen.

Proper 10

(Sunday between July 10 and July 16 inclusive)

COMPLEMENTARY

Deuteronomy 30:9–14	Colossians 1:1–14
Psalm 25:1–10	Luke 10:25–37

OPENING WORDS / CALL TO WORSHIP

All the paths of the Lord *Ps. 25:10*
are steadfast love and faithfulness
for those who keep God's covenants.
God leads the humble in what is right
and teaches them God's way.

CALL TO CONFESSION

[Water may be poured into the baptismal font.]
The God who demands justice from us
is the God who pours out mercy upon us.
Trusting in that gracious love,
let us confess our sin before God and one another.

PRAYER OF CONFESSION

God of Mercy: *Luke 10:29*
We confess that we have failed to live
as your beloved sons and daughters.
We have set our minds on the things of this world,
and we have neglected the inheritance of love
you bestow upon your saints.
We have pursued selfish aims in our daily business;
we have harbored uncharitable thoughts
toward our enemies and friends;
we have avoided difficult responsibilities to
our neighbors.
Forgive us, we pray.

87

Free us from our selfish ways
and strengthen us to be faithful disciples of Jesus Christ,
in whose name we pray. Amen.

DECLARATION OF FORGIVENESS

Hear the good news:
Christ is merciful to all who turn to him in repentance.
In the name of Jesus Christ, we are forgiven.
Thanks be to God.

PRAYER OF THE DAY

Give your church, O God,   *Luke 10:25–37*
the grace to serve you with courage,
that our lives may be a witness to your compassion
and our actions a testimony to your mercy.
Though Jesus Christ our Lord,
by the power of the Holy Spirit, we pray. **Amen.**

PRAYER FOR ILLUMINATION

O God, as we receive your Word
through your Holy Spirit,
open our eyes to your justice,
open our ears to your judgment,
open our hearts to your love. **Amen.**

PRAYERS OF INTERCESSION

In peace, let us pray to the Lord, saying,
hear our prayer.   *Luke 10:25–37; Col. 1:10*

Gracious God,
you know our wounds, our troubles, and our needs
even before we know them ourselves.
As the Samaritan showed compassion to the wounded man,
you offer mercy to us.

We pray for those who are sick or in trouble (especially *N.*).
Comfort them with your grace,
and empower your church to minister to them.
God of Compassion, **hear our prayer.**

We pray for all who suffer the violence of human hands
or the tragedy of natural disaster (especially *N.*).
Shield them with your holy angels,
and motivate your church to care for them.
God of Compassion, **hear our prayer.**

We pray for children and for the defenseless.
Safeguard them in your protection,
and strengthen your church to tend to them.
God of Compassion, **hear our prayer.**

We pray for elected officials and for civil servants.
Stir them to heed justice,
and rouse the church to hold them accountable.
God of Compassion, **hear our prayer.**

We pray for pastors, teachers, musicians, *[bishops, etc.],*
and all the saints who lead your church.
Inspire them by your Holy Spirit,
and guide the church to encourage them.
God of Compassion, **hear our prayer.**

God of Compassion, receive our prayers,
and lead us all to serve in love,
through Christ our Lord. **Amen.**

INVITATION TO THE OFFERING
Let us bring to God the fruit of our labors.

PRAYER OF THANKSGIVING/DEDICATION
Receive these gifts, O God.   *Col. 1:9–10*
May our lives be an offering that is pleasing to you,
good gifts that come from the knowledge of life in
    Christ our Lord,
in whose name we pray. **Amen.**

CHARGE
Go forth to share the light of God's compassion with
    all the world,   *Col. 1:12*
for God has given us the inheritance of the saints.

BLESSING

The grace of Christ,
the love of God,
and the fellowship of the Spirit be with you.

Questions for Reflection

How does the story of the compassionate Samaritan expand your
understanding of who your neighbor may be? With whom do you identify
most in this parable?

Household Prayer: Morning

Arouse my heart, O God, to your love,
and let me love my neighbor
with the same consideration I desire for myself.
Through Christ I pray. Amen.

Household Prayer: Evening

O God, you have held me and cared for my wounded soul
in ways I may not have been aware.
Let me now rest from the labors of this day,
secure in your love.
Through Christ I pray. Amen.

Proper 11

(Sunday between July 17 and July 23 inclusive)

SEMICONTINUOUS

Amos 8:1–12	Colossians 1:15–28
Psalm 52	Luke 10:38–42

OPENING WORDS / CALL TO WORSHIP

God is good and loving to the faithful.
Give thanks and praise for all that God has done for us.
God is good! Praise the Lord!

CALL TO CONFESSION

We live with this reality:
God never forgets what we have done
but, in mercy, forgives
those whose hearts are full of repentance.
Let us confess those things
that break our relationship with God,
assured that God will never break relationship with us.

PRAYER OF CONFESSION

*[Consider having two voices pray the first two paragraphs
of this prayer, with the entire assembly speaking
the final paragraph.]*
Sometimes, O God, we behave like Martha.   *Luke 10:38–42*
We get distracted in our routines,
so busy with our daily chores
that we forget to take the time
to stop and breathe,
to look up and to notice the creation you have given
and the way it speaks about your love and passion
for your people.
We do not take time to listen for your words,

while reading the Bible,
while listening to music,
while talking to friends,
and we become worried and upset about many things.

Sometimes, O God, we behave like Mary.
We devote our time to looking up,
thinking that everything we are commanded to do
is to love God, and we forget
to serve our neighbor,
and to commit our time to
the concrete work of the church,
forgetting to get our hands dirty.

God of balance, help us:
forgive us when we do not know
when to be workers
and when to be hearers.
In your mercy, heal our worries
and our judgments,
so that we can, indeed,
keep the best part.
In the name of our loving Master. Amen.

DECLARATION OF FORGIVENESS
Before,
because of your evil thoughts and actions,
you were strangers and enemies of God.
Now,
you have been reconciled to God
by the death and resurrection of Christ.
Now,
you can live in peace,
restored by the blood
shed on the cross.
Live thankfully!
In Jesus Christ we are forgiven!
Thanks be to God!

PRAYER OF THE DAY

Grant us this day, O God,
not to be overtaken by anxious thoughts
that can make us feel that you are not near.
Give us the chance,
to sit at your feet,
to enjoy every word and every musical note
that we may feel your real presence
and in turn live out that presence
within our families, our communities,
our jobs, and our schools.
Prepare us as we journey
as your people,
to worship and to obey.
Through Jesus Christ our Lord,
the image of the invisible God,
and the firstborn over all creation. **Amen.**

PRAYER FOR ILLUMINATION

Open our hearts and our minds,
so that we can understand the fullness of your Word.
Fill us with the light of the Holy Spirit,
and bless the servant you have chosen,
to share the Word proclaimed today.
In the name of Christ, the Word revealed. **Amen.**

PRAYERS OF INTERCESSION

Creator God, as we look at the world you have made,
we notice that the songs of love that you wanted us to sing
have turned into cries of abuse, oppression, and prejudice.

We have abused the planet that you have provided
for us to inhabit and to share with other creatures.
We have wasted the water, abused other resources,
limited access to food, and marked borders of inhospitality.
We pray for this world in need of restoration
and ask that you provide us with the tools and the intelligence
needed to rebuild the world you created for us.

God, save us, heal us, and make us whole.

There is oppression in the world that we live in.
We see it in the ways human beings treat one another,
taking advantage of those considered to be of less value.
We turn our eyes away when we see the needy being trampled
or the poor being stashed out of sight.
May your will be the last word,
and the church an effective witness
to the Sovereign Lord in our midst.

God, save us, heal us, and make us whole.

We see prejudice in our relationships, Lord.
We judge one another,
not with justice and fairness,
but with fear and misinformation.
It is easier to demonize
than to take the time to listen
and to establish relationships.
It is easier to assume
than to ask questions and to acquire knowledge.
Make us agents of peace
and restore our songs of love
for you and for one another.

God, save us, heal us, and make us whole. Amen.

INVITATION TO THE OFFERING
Bring your gifts and your talents,
bring your sacrifice of praise to the Lord.
Bring them with prayers and shouts of thanksgiving,
to celebrate God's faithfulness!

PRAYER OF THANKSGIVING/DEDICATION
[May be spoken by one or by all.]
God, we give today in thankfulness
and with the assurance that
anything we give will contribute
to the continuing growth
of your kingdom in the world.
Give us wisdom as a church,

so that this offering is used
for the sharing of your word
and the service of your people.
In the name of the One that gave us
everything we are and have. **Amen.**

CHARGE

Go out into the world
proclaiming Christ in every corner,
admonishing and teaching with all wisdom,
so that everyone can comprehend fully
the presence and witness of Christ,
by the power of the Holy Spirit.

BLESSING

Receive the blessing of God,
whose mercy knows no ends.

Receive the blessing of Christ,
who is patient and eager to give us words of life.

Receive the blessing of the Holy Spirit
who moves us and gives us power
to do God's will.

Receive the blessing of the triune God,
and share this blessing with others!

Question for Reflection

How do you balance studying the Word and fostering a relationship with
God while also serving others?

Household Prayer: Morning

God, we have too many things to do today!
Help us to see you in everything we do,
in everything we say.
Help us to take a deep breath
and to remember that the Holy Spirit
is inside us, with us, around us.

Help us to pause and drink a glass of water,
and to remember our baptism,
and the covenant you have established,
making us your children.
Help us to study your Word,
and not to think just of the past,
but also of how you act in the present.
And help us to work for and with
our brothers and sisters,
giving kindness, sharing hope,
and living out the faith you have given us. Amen.

Household Prayer: Evening

Today, O Lord,
we have sat at your feet.
and listened to your words.
We have been empowered
by your teachings.
What should we do with all this life
that you have provided?
We will go out into the world,
after a restful night,
and serve, and smile, and love,
and work, and play, and forgive,
and shout out, and sing, . . .
doing everything in your name! Amen.

Proper 11

(Sunday between July 17 and July 23 inclusive)

COMPLEMENTARY

Genesis 18:1–10a	Colossians 1:15–28
Psalm 15	Luke 10:38–42

OPENING WORDS / CALL TO WORSHIP

In Jesus Christ   *Col. 1:19–22*
all the fullness of God was pleased to dwell.
Through him God was reconciled to all things
in heaven and on earth,
even to us,
that we might be holy and blameless before God.
In awe and gratitude,
let us worship the Lord our God.

CALL TO CONFESSION

With humble and trusting hearts,
let us confess our sins before God and one another.

PRAYER OF CONFESSION

Merciful God,   *Luke 10:41*
we confess that we have been distracted with
 many things
and have not loved you with our whole heart
 and strength.
We have not paid attention to your Word.
We have allowed the poor to be neglected and the
 weak to be oppressed.
We have been impatient in worship and insincere in
 our dealings with others.
We have ignored signs of injustice and disregarded
 warnings of judgment.
Forgive us, we pray, and teach us repentance.

Free us from our habits of pride,
and make us steadfast in faith,
that we may live as those who are reconciled with you
in Jesus Christ our Lord, with whom we pray. Amen.

DECLARATION OF FORGIVENESS

Though we were once estranged,
in Jesus Christ we have been reconciled with God.
Baptized, forgiven, and freed,
we are one with the Lord and with each other.
Thanks be to God! **Amen.**

PRAYER OF THE DAY

Almighty God,   *Col. 1:16–23*
you brought creation into being through Christ,
and in Christ all things find their purpose.
Open our eyes to see the world as your gift
and to use your gifts for the sake of Christ,
that through the witness of our lives
the gospel may be proclaimed to all people. **Amen.**

PRAYER FOR ILLUMINATION

O God, as the Scriptures are read and the gospel proclaimed,
open our ears to hear your Word,
open our eyes to see your truth,
and open our hearts to receive your grace. **Amen.**

PRAYERS OF INTERCESSION

In peace let us pray to the Lord saying,   *Col. 1:22–23*
Lord have mercy.

For the church throughout the world,
that we may follow Christ our Head,
and be blameless in living the gospel of reconciliation,
let us pray to the Lord.
Lord have mercy.

For the nations of the world,
that all may live without fear of oppression, poverty, or war,
let us pray to the Lord.
Lord have mercy.

For the earth,
that we may wisely use its resources
for the benefit of humankind
and offer help wherever natural disaster has fractured human trust
in the goodness of creation, especially *[name a place of recent disaster]*,
let us pray to the Lord.
Lord have mercy.

For the leaders of the nations *[for President N., etc.]*,
that they may honor justice,
protect the weak,
and serve the common good,
let us pray to the Lord.
Lord have mercy.

For our communities and neighborhoods,
that all may dwell in harmony,
let us pray to the Lord.
Lord have mercy.

For our enemies,
that we may find reconciliation with them
for the sake of Christ,
let us pray to the Lord.
Lord have mercy.

For all who are sick and in trouble, especially *N.*,
that they may find healing and peace,
let us pray to the Lord.
Lord have mercy.

Merciful God,
hear the prayers of your people,
offered in steadfast faith and hope in your care for us.
For we ask these things in the name of Jesus Christ, our Lord. **Amen.**

INVITATION TO THE OFFERING
In gratitude for all that God has done for us,
let us present our gifts to God.

PRAYER OF THANKSGIVING/DEDICATION

O God,
receive these gifts, which are the product of our labors,   *Luke 10:42*
and let us not forget the better part of our offering,
which is our devotion to the words of life
we have received from Christ our Lord. **Amen.**

CHARGE

Go in peace.

BLESSING

The God of reconciliation bless you,
the grace of our Lord Jesus Christ keep you,
and the power of the Holy Spirit strengthen you
this day and forevermore.

Questions for Reflection

What is the meaning of service? Martha was serving Jesus by being a
gracious host and providing a meal. Mary was not serving, but listening to
Jesus' teaching. Jesus commends Mary's attentiveness to his teaching and
gently rebukes Martha for her busyness in serving. He says, "there is need
of only one thing." What is that "one thing" of which Jesus speaks?

Household Prayer: Morning

Dear God, as I begin this day
I renew my commitment to live
as an agent of your reconciling love.
Keep my actions holy,
my thoughts blameless,
and my intentions irreproachable.
Let me be firm in the hope
promised by the gospel,
that my life may bear witness to Jesus Christ my Lord. Amen.

Household Prayer: Evening

Lord Jesus,
the labors of the day are over

and the evening rest begins.
If I have been busy with too many things,
return my thoughts to what is needful.
At last, let me know the better part you have promised
will not be taken away,
that I may sleep in your peace
and awaken with renewed attentiveness to your presence. Amen.

Proper 12

(*Sunday between July 24 and July 30 inclusive*)

SEMICONTINUOUS

Hosea 1:2–10   Colossians 2:6–15 (16–19)
Psalm 85   Luke 11:1–13

OPENING WORDS / CALL TO WORSHIP
Show us your steadfast love, O Lord,   *Ps. 85:7–9*
and grant us your salvation.
The Lord will speak peace to the faithful,
to those who turn to God in their hearts.
Surely salvation is at hand for those who fear the Lord,
and God's glory will dwell in our land.

CALL TO CONFESSION
[spoken from the font]
The truth about us is this:
we all sin and fall short of the glory of God.
Yet God promises to pour out grace upon us,
giving us confidence to show ourselves as we are
and be freed from shame.
Trusting in God's mercy,
let us confess our sin before God and one another.

PRAYER OF CONFESSION
Ever-faithful God,   *Hos. 1:2*
how often we turn away from you,
yet you remain constant to us.
We run from you, but you call us back.
In our words and our deeds we dishonor you,
yet you still profess your love for us.
We cut ourselves off from you and from others,   *Col. 2:19*
but you will not let us go.

**Forgive our faithless and fickle ways
and increase our gratitude,
that we might grow in faithfulness to you,
for the sake of Jesus Christ,
in whose name we pray. Amen.**

DECLARATION OF FORGIVENESS

Hear the good news!
[Water is poured into the font, visibly and audibly.]
When you were buried with Christ in baptism,   *Col. 2:12*
you were also raised with him through faith in the
    power of God.
By that power we are made clean
and set free
to live in gratitude and love with zeal.

As you have received Christ Jesus,   *Col. 2:6–7*
continue to live your lives in him,
rooted and built up in him
and abounding in thanksgiving.

PRAYER OF THE DAY

Holy God,
you are our faithful lover,
our generous parent,
our patient teacher,
our constant friend.
We live by the hope of your promises,
seek to follow your way,
and rely on the gift of your Spirit,
by whose power we breathe, and move, and pray. **Amen.**

PRAYER FOR ILLUMINATION

God of Wisdom,
you promise to give your Spirit to those who ask.   *Luke 11:13*
Overwhelm us with your Word,
that we may know you more fully,
love you more passionately,
and follow you more closely;
in Jesus' name we pray. **Amen.**

PRAYERS OF INTERCESSION

God knows us better than we know ourselves.
Relying on the Spirit, let us pray for the needs of the world, saying,
God of mercy, hear our prayer.

For your whole, hurting, hating world:
[silence]
Lead us in the ways of peace,
especially in places where tyrants reign
and people eat the bread of conflict every day.
God of mercy, **hear our prayer.**

For your church, whose body is strong in some places,
    and frail in others:
[silence]
Nourish your church in the world, O Lord,
that those who are flourishing might proclaim your word with power,
and those who are weak might be strengthened to do your work.
God of mercy, **hear our prayer.**

For your earth, that suffers at the hands of your own people:
[silence]
Pour out your healing mercy on this planet you have made,
and prod us to be worthy stewards of its beauty and its gifts,
that in honoring the earth we may also honor you.
God of mercy, **hear our prayer.**

For those who suffer because of disease or injury,
the addicted, the abused, the feeble, and the ill:
[silence]
Soothe our suffering and heal our wounds.
Protect us from evil and calm our anxious hearts.
Make us whole in you.
God of mercy, **hear our prayer.**

For those who are dying and the ones who care for them:
[silence]
Receive them into your arms of mercy
and welcome them into the company of the saints in light.
God of mercy, **hear our prayer.**

For all those whose burdens we carry in our hearts,
and those known only to you:
[silence]
Bestow your good gifts as you see fit,
supplying every need by the power of your Spirit.
Accept all these prayers we offer in faith,
even as you continue to teach us to pray
through Jesus Christ our Lord. **Amen.**

INVITATION TO THE OFFERING

As we wait for the coming of God's good reign,
we answer the invitation to take part in God's work,
bringing our tithes and offerings
with joyful gratitude.

PRAYER OF THANKSGIVING/DEDICATION

Lord, you are the giver of every good gift.   *Mic. 6:8*
Accept these offerings we pray,
that through them we may do justice,
and love kindness,
and walk humbly with you,
our Sovereign and our God.

CHARGE

Steadfast love and faithfulness will meet;   *Ps. 85:10*
righteousness and peace will kiss each other.
Go in peace, confident in the promises of God.

BLESSING

May the grace of Christ attend you,
the love of God surround you,
and the Holy Spirit keep you,
this day and forevermore.

Questions for Reflection

It is difficult in our day to consider the analogy of Hosea and Gomer (Hos. 1:2–10). The figure of Gomer as adulterous prostitute offends our feminist sensibilities, and Hosea evokes pity more than admiration. Yet, as William Willimon points out, this scandalous story directs our attention to the God who went so far as to be crucified for us. "Only a passionate, unseemly God who is willing to risk scandal could possibly save a bunch of adulterers like us."* What does it mean to place ourselves in the role of Gomer? What does the person Hosea say about the character of God?

Household Prayer: Morning

Thank you, God of light, for waking me up this morning.
May I live wholly for you this day,
that whatever I say and do might help make a path for your coming reign.
Open my eyes to your goodness and my heart to your children.
I pray in Jesus' name. Amen.

Household Prayer: Evening

Thank you, Lord, for the gift of this day,
its challenges and its blessings,
its burdens and its delights.
Forgive my failures and misdeeds
and refine my heart,
that I may greet the new day to live more faithfully for you. Amen.

*William H. Willimon, "Pastoral Perspective" on Hosea 1:2–10, Proper 12, in *Feasting on the Word: Preaching the Revised Common Lectionary, Year C, Volume 3*, ed. David L. Bartlett and Barbara Brown Taylor (Louisville, KY: Westminster John Knox Press, 2010), 272.

Proper 12

(Sunday between July 24 and July 30 inclusive)

COMPLEMENTARY

Genesis 18:20–32   Colossians 2:6–15 (16–19)
Psalm 138   Luke 11:1–13

OPENING WORDS / CALL TO WORSHIP

The Prophet Isaiah wrote, Hear the word of the LORD,
you rulers of Sodom!   *Isa. 1:10–17*
My soul hates your worship mixed with
your hypocrisy!
Instead, learn to
do good and seek justice:
rescue the oppressed,
defend the orphans, and
treat the widows fairly!

The Prophet Ezekiel wrote, Thus says the LORD,
God of Israel: *Ezek. 16:49*
This was the guilt of Sodom:
they were arrogant,
they had prosperous ease and excess of food,
and yet they did not aid the poor and the needy.

The Prophet Amos wrote: Thus says the LORD—
hear this Word: *Amos 4:1, 11*
You who oppress the poor and crush the needy . . .
I shall overthrow you as I overthrew Sodom
and Gomorrah.

Matthew and Luke both report that,   *Matt. 10:15;*
when Jesus sent the disciples out two-by-two   *Luke 10:12*
to spread the good news,
he said to them,

If any town does not show you hospitality,
shake the dust of that town off your sandals and leave—
it will be worse for them than it was for Sodom.

God of Love and Justice,
turn our hearts toward doing good and seeking justice.
Ignite us to rescue the oppressed,
defend the orphans,
and help the widows,
for the sake of Jesus Christ our Lord.

CALL TO CONFESSION

Let us turn to the most Holy One and confess our sin,   *Ps. 138:2*
confident in God's faithful and steadfast love for us.

PRAYER OF CONFESSION

Holy One, although we come to church on Sundays,   *Luke 11:1*
we too often live the rest of the week as though
     you don't exist.
We act as though we created ourselves,
with no connection to you,
with no hope of transcendence.

Open us to your constant presence, Holy One.
Teach us to pray,
and restore our sight,
that we may commune with you each day
in the light of eternity. Amen.

DECLARATION OF FORGIVENESS

Hear this from God's Word: Neither death nor life,
     powers nor rulers,
things present nor future, nor anything else in
     all creation
can separate us from the love of God in Christ Jesus.   *Rom. 8:38*
Therefore do not let anyone condemn you
or disqualify you from the body,
but hold fast to its head, who nourishes growth
     from God.   *Col. 2:16–19*
And let the peace of Christ rule in your hearts.   *Col.3:15*

PRAYER OF THE DAY

Jesus Christ, teach us to pray,   *Luke 11:1, 13;*
and to trust the hospitality of God for   *Exod. 16:14*
  our daily bread,
as our ancestors who ate manna in the wilderness.
Let us likewise be hospitable,
and as God gives the gift of the Holy Spirit to us,
let us give good gifts to those who are in need. **Amen.**

PRAYER FOR ILLUMINATION

God of Love and Justice,   *Col. 2:8, 10;*
we are grateful for inheriting the tradition of   *John 1:14*
  the Scriptures.
By your Holy Spirit, speak to us through your Word,
that we may know the love and grace of Jesus Christ,
your living Word made flesh among us.

PRAYERS OF INTERCESSION

O God most high, you care for the lowly, but look
  down on the haughty.   *Ps. 138:6*
In your steadfast love, fulfill your purpose for us.   *Ps. 138:8*
Restore us again, O God of our salvation.   *Ps. 85:4*
We pray for the church and for all who work to
  give hospitality to others.
Restore us again, O God of our salvation.
We pray for peace among nations, religions, ideologies,
  and people.
Restore us again, O God of our salvation.
We pray for those injured by war, natural disaster,
  or financial collapse,
all who cry out for help.
Restore us again, O God of our salvation.
We pray for those oppressed because of class, age, gender,
  ability, or sexual orientation.
Restore us again, O God of our salvation.
We pray for those afflicted by illness
or overcome by the fear of death.
Restore us again, O God of our salvation.
Gracious God, you are the friend of those in need.   *Luke 11:5*
Like Abraham and Sarah, may we show you hospitality,   *Gen. 18:1*

whether you come in the form of angels or strangers,   *Heb. 13:2*
for the sake of Jesus Christ, our Lord. **Amen.**

INVITATION TO THE OFFERING
Jesus teaches us that if we ask, it will be
 given to us.   *Luke 11:9; Ps. 138:8*
Let us participate in God's purpose, then,
 by giving generously
for all who are in need.

PRAYER OF THANKSGIVING/DEDICATION
Holy One, we give you thanks for your steadfast love
 and faithfulness.   *Ps. 138:1*
Bless these offerings and transform them into gifts
 of hospitality
for those who need them most. **Amen.**

CHARGE
Ask, and it will be given to you;
search, and you will find;   *Luke 11:9*
knock, and the door will be opened to you.

BLESSING
May God preserve you,
protect and keep you,
this day and for all eternity.

Question for Reflection

This week's lectionary texts all say that the sins of Sodom and Gomorrah
were arrogance, excess food and leisure, injustice and inhospitality,
and not helping the poor and oppressed. Why do you think rich and
powerful church leaders in the Middle Ages and in modern times went
against the Bible and taught that the sin of Sodom and Gomorrah was
"homosexuality" (a word not invented until the late nineteenth century)?

Household Prayer: Morning

God, as this new day begins, I imagine Abraham sitting
    in the shade
under his oak tree when you appeared to him in the form
    of three strangers
and he offered them hospitality.   *Gen. 18:1–5*
Help me to see opportunities to extend hospitality to
    those in need today,
even if it's as small a gesture as offering someone a cup
    of cold water. Amen.   *Matt. 10:42*

Household Prayer: Evening

I return to you, God, as this day ends.
I am grateful for all that you have given me,
all that I have found,
and all the doors that were opened to me.   *Luke 11:9*
As for those prayers that seem as yet unanswered,
I leave them with you for now
and turn to my rest in the gift of your Holy Spirit. Amen.   *Luke 11:13*

Proper 13

(Sunday between July 31 and August 6 inclusive)

SEMICONTINUOUS

Hosea 11:1–11	Colossians 3:1–11
Psalm 107:1–9, 43	Luke 12:13–21

OPENING WORDS / CALL TO WORSHIP
We are children of God, learning to walk.   *Hos. 11:3–4*
Day by day, we are learning to be the church.
God is a loving parent, teaching us to walk.
God loves us, leads us, and feeds us.

CALL TO CONFESSION
Let us return to our God in confession,   *Ps. 107:43*
considering God's steadfast love.

PRAYER OF CONFESSION
**Nurturing God, you continue to lead us
    in upright ways**   *Ps. 107:7; Hos.11:1–11*
on account of your love for us.
Yet we do not always follow your call;
we turn away from you and go our own way.
Forgive us,
and return us to our rightful home in you,
through Jesus Christ our Savior. Amen.

DECLARATION OF FORGIVENESS
Hear these words from our God: *Hos. 11:8–11*
I cannot give up on you—
my compassion grows warm and tender.
When my children come trembling,
I will bring them home.
Believe the gospel.
In Jesus Christ, we are forgiven.

PRAYER OF THE DAY

Holy One, you see us for just who we are,   *Hos. 11:1, 4*
and yet you love us with a parent's love.
In your enduring love for us,
we see both our guilt and our acquittal.
Gracious God,
continue to guide us and teach us to walk in your ways.
In the name of Jesus we pray. **Amen.**

PRAYER FOR ILLUMINATION

God, we trust that you have our best interests at heart.   *Col. 3:1*
As we hear the reading of your Word,
remind us that we have been raised with Christ,
and inspire us to seek the things that are above,
through the power of your Holy Spirit. **Amen.**

PRAYERS OF INTERCESSION

Loving God, we are much in need   *Hos. 11:2–4; Pss. 49:2;*
   of your guidance.   *107:43; Luke 12:18*
When we wobble and fall, stand us up and
   help us walk again
with cords of human kindness and bands of love.
**I am to them like those who lift their infants to
   their cheeks.**
We pray for the church and for all who teach others
with kindness, firm guidance, and love.
**I am to them like those who lift their infants to
   their cheeks.**
We pray for peace among nations and peace between
   people.
**I am to them like those who lift their infants to
   their cheeks.**
We pray for those suffering the scourge of war and
   the calamities of nature.
**I am to them like those who lift their infants to
   their cheeks.**
We pray for all those in need,
especially women and children who suffer domestic
   violence and homelessness.

**I am to them like those who lift their infants to
their cheeks.**

We pray for those who are ill, their families, and
their caregivers.

**I am to them like those who lift their infants to
their cheeks.**

We pray for those who refuse to give, who have
more than enough

but choose to build new barns in which to hoard
instead of help.

**I am to them like those who lift their infants
to their cheeks.**

Loving God, through Jesus Christ you nurture
and nourish us.

You love us with a steadfast love: low and high,
rich and poor together.

Renew in us your call and release us from all fear,

that we may heed these things and consider your
steadfast love for all. **Amen.**

INVITATION TO THE OFFERING

Through Jesus Christ, God cautions us against   *Luke 12:21*
storing up riches for ourselves.

Let us consider these things and give as our conscience
directs us.

PRAYER OF THANKSGIVING/DEDICATION

Holy One, we give you thanks for the richness of
our lives.

Bless these tithes and offerings,

that they might be used as expressions of your
steadfast love

for those in need near and far. **Amen.**

CHARGE

Remember, you never know when your life will be
demanded of you.   *Luke 12:20*

So do not be a fool who stores up riches for yourself,
but is poor toward God.

BLESSING

Now may we be raised with Christ into the things
    that are above.   *Col. 3:1, 9–11*
May we strip off our old selves and clothe ourselves
    in the new self
that is renewed in the image of its creator.
And may we find our home in the community of
    the Holy Spirit
where there is no longer Jew and Gentile, religious
    and unreligious,
conservative and liberal, rich and poor,
but where Christ is all and in all!

Questions for Reflection

Sometimes divine love includes judgment. But the judgment of God is love. What do you think might be the only way that we can be rejected or separated from that divine love? Would God be rejecting us, or would we be rejecting God's love?

Household Prayer: Morning

Loving God, as I embark on the adventure of this new day,
I will imagine you as my mother or father,
teaching me to walk with cords of human kindness and love,
a tether as you guide me along.
Therefore I will not fear failure
or worry that I will not have enough time or goods
if I give a little to those in need. Amen.

Household Prayer: Evening

Thank you, God, for the gift of this day.
Thank you for bringing me home to you.
As I fall asleep, I will consider your steadfast love for me
and repeat with my breathing,
"You are rich toward me, and I am rich toward you.
You are rich toward me, and I am rich toward you." Amen.

Proper 13

COMPLEMENTARY

Ecclesiastes 1:2, 12–14; 2:18–23   Colossians 3:1–11
Psalm 49:1–12   Luke 12:13–21

OPENING WORDS / CALL TO WORSHIP
Sisters and brothers,
we have been raised with Christ to new life,
freed from every fear,
and granted every grace.
With songs of praise, let us worship God.

CALL TO CONFESSION
Already assured that forgiveness is ours in Jesus Christ,
let us lay aside every weight   *Heb. 12:1*
and the sin that clings so closely,
that we might receive mercy and amend our lives.

PRAYER OF CONFESSION
Holy God,
you lavish us with good gifts,
yet we persist in seeking after that
which robs us of abundant life.
We hold fast to our anxieties
and give in to our greed;
we desire the very things that harm us.
Forgive us, purify us,
and sustain us by the strength of your Holy Spirit,
we ask in Jesus' name. Amen.

DECLARATION OF FORGIVENESS
If God is for us, who is against us?   *Rom. 8:31*
In Jesus Christ you have been set free.
Know that you are forgiven, and be at peace.

PRAYER OF THE DAY

Extravagant God,
you offer riches that no earthly pleasures can match.
You pour out mercy and cover us with love.
You show us true justice and offer us peace.
You provide us with every need
and promise us eternal life with you.
In the midst of the glitz and glamour of this world,
nothing, and no one, shines with your brilliance.
Bathe us in the light of Christ,
illumine us with your Holy Spirit,
and enable us to live only for you.
In Jesus' name we pray. **Amen.**

PRAYER FOR ILLUMINATION

Holy God,
allow us your wisdom.
By the power of your Holy Spirit
open the Scriptures to us today,
that in the Word read and proclaimed
we might know your truth.
In Jesus' name we ask it. **Amen.**

PRAYERS OF INTERCESSION

[A time of silence follows each intercession.]
God of heaven and earth,
in your wisdom you made the whole creation
and called it good.
You have lavished your creatures
with beauty and sustained us with your grace.
Even so, we are distracted and seduced
and wreak havoc on the world you made.
Humbly, then, we pray to you for
comfort and healing and peace, saying,
Gracious God, hear our prayer.

For those who declare war, those who wage it, and those who
suffer from it . . .
Gracious God, **hear our prayer.**
For your church, that we may overcome divisions and live in
the unity given to us in Christ . . .
Gracious God, **hear our prayer.**

For your creation, that the earth's wounds may be healed
and we may become better caretakers . . .
  Gracious God, **hear our prayer.**
For those who fight despair, struggle with addiction,
    or live without hope . . .
  Gracious God, **hear our prayer.**
For those who are ill, and all who care for them . . .
  Gracious God, **hear our prayer.**
For the secret burdens of our hearts . . .
  Gracious God, **hear our prayer.**

Grateful for your mercy,
we entrust these and all our prayers to you,
through our Savior Jesus Christ,
in whose name we pray. **Amen.**

INVITATION TO THE OFFERING
God pours out blessings upon us,
not so we can hoard them or take pride in what we have
but that we might share our goods with the same generous spirit.
With joy, let us bring our tithes and offerings to God.

PRAYER OF THANKSGIVING/DEDICATION
All we have and all we are comes from you, O God,
our Father, our Mother, our Creator, our Sovereign.
If we were to give thanks until the end of time,
we could not repay your benevolence and grace.
Take these meager offerings, we pray,
and increase our generosity,
that everything we say and do
might show forth your irrepressible love.
Through Jesus Christ our Lord. **Amen.**

CHARGE
Since you have been raised with Christ   *Col. 3:1–2*
seek the things that are of God,
and go forth to live lives worthy of your calling.

BLESSING

May the God who gives us every good gift
bless you and keep you in the mind of Christ,
by the power of the Spirit who sustains us all. **Amen.**

Question for Reflection

The Christian life is one of constant renewal, turning and returning to God.
In this season of your life, what would it mean to strip off the old self with
its practices and clothe yourself with the new self (Col. 3:9–10)?

Household Prayer: Morning

I greet this new day with joy, O Lord,
for you are my light and my hope.
Do not let me fall prey to the anxieties
of this world,
or be tempted by false charms,
but keep me ever faithful to you,
for Jesus' sake. Amen.

Household Prayer: Evening

Holy Comforter, Protector, and Deliverer,
at the close of this day I entrust to you
all my life and all those I hold dear,
knowing that your tender mercies
cover all my failings and all my fears.
Thank you for your unending love. Amen.

Proper 14

SEMICONTINUOUS

Isaiah 1:1, 10–20   Hebrews 11:1–3, 8–16
Psalm 50:1–8, 22–23   Luke 12:32–40

OPENING WORDS / CALL TO WORSHIP

The heavens declare the righteousness of God.   *Ps. 50:1–2*
The earth declares God's beauty.
From the rising of the sun to its setting
God's word shines forth in glory.

CALL TO CONFESSION

My brothers and sisters, remember that God loves us;   *Isa. 1:16–17*
therefore by the mercy of God,
let us cease to do evil and learn to do good.

PRAYER OF CONFESSION

Holy God, you call us to do good,   *Isa. 1:17*
seek justice, and care for those in need,
yet how often we place our own comforts
above compassion for others.
Forgive us, we pray,
and cleanse us from these and all our offenses
through Jesus Christ our Lord. Amen.

DECLARATION OF FORGIVENESS

God is merciful and kind;   *Isa. 1:16–18*
though our sins are like scarlet,
    they become like snow.
Be at peace,
for your sins are washed clean by the goodness
    of God.

PRAYER OF THE DAY

O God of promise, creator of the cosmos, *Luke 12:35–40*
you are the first light breaking through the void,
and the final light we shall eternally enjoy.
Keep our hearts ever vigilant
as we wait to welcome you,
that you would find us clothed in love,
dressed for action, and eager to receive you. **Amen.**

PRAYER FOR ILLUMINATION

God of Hope, *Heb. 11:1, 3*
by faith we know that you created the world,
and that what is seen is made by things that are not visible.
Open our eyes to your presence among us
that we may hear your word with clarity
and a sureness of hope,
as we follow you in all righteousness.
Through Jesus Christ, our Lord. **Amen.**

PRAYERS OF INTERCESSION

Let us pray for the world, saying,
O God of hope, increase our faith.
[The leader may gesture to the assembly to indicate the response.]

O God, your blessings are as plentiful as the
  stars above *Heb. 11; Ps. 33*
and as numerous as the grains of sand along
  the seashore,
we come before you with grateful hearts
as we pray for the church and the world, saying,
O God of hope,
increase our faith.

We pray for wisdom and guidance
for all people and leaders of this world,
that they may foster peace and justice
and serve the common good.
O God of hope,
increase our faith.

We pray for your church,
that by your grace and our faith
we may serve you with constancy and love.
O God of hope,
increase our faith.

We pray for those who are sick or suffer any need,
that they would know your healing strength
and find comfort through our faithful care.
O God of hope,
increase our faith.

Help us to protect the goodness of your creation,
that all may enjoy the precious blessings of this world
as foretaste of the next.
O God of hope,
increase our faith.

We remember those who have died
and look to that heavenly city
where with you and all your saints
we will enter the everlasting heritage
of your faithful sons and daughters.
O God of hope,
increase our faith.

Holy God, steadfast and true,
on you our hope is founded.
Receive the prayers of your faithful people
for our hearts are gladdened by our trust in you. **Amen.**

INVITATION TO THE OFFERING

Jesus said, "Sell your possessions, and
   give alms.
For where your treasure is, there your
   heart will be also."
Honor God with a sacrifice of thanksgiving
and come into God's courts with praise.

Luke 12:33a, 34;
Ps. 50:23

PRAYER OF THANKSGIVING/DEDICATION

Lord, you look down from heaven,   *Ps. 33:13; Gen.15:5;*
see all humankind, and long to call   *Heb.11:14*
    us home.
Accept these gifts on behalf of your people,
that they would increase faith,
nurture hope,
and be reckoned as righteous in your sight. **Amen.**

CHARGE

Be dressed for action and ready to serve,   *Luke 12:35, 40*
for the Son of Man is coming at an unexpected hour.

BLESSING

Be not afraid,   *Luke 12:32–33*
for it is God's good pleasure to give you the kingdom,
an unfailing treasure and eternal blessing.

Questions for Reflection

What does it mean to be ready for Christ's coming? In what sense is the
coming of the kingdom like "a thief in the night" (Luke 12:39)?

Household Prayer: Morning

Holy God, at your word the sun rises to greet us,
and we are new each morning.
Be with me as I begin this day,
that my faith would be reckoned righteous by you,
and my works find favor in your sight. Amen.

Household Prayer: Evening

Holy God,
at the setting of the sun your love brings judgment,
and I know of my need for your grace.
Help me to be more faithful to justice,
more truthful in love,
and ever mindful of your mercy. Amen.

Proper 14

(Sunday between August 7 and August 13 inclusive)

COMPLEMENTARY

Genesis 15:1–6   Hebrews 11:1–3, 8–16
Psalm 33:12–22   Luke 12:32–40

OPENING WORDS / CALL TO WORSHIP
Our soul waits for the Lord, who is our help
    and shield.   *Ps. 33:20–22*
**Our hearts are glad, because we trust in God's
    holy name.**
Let your steadfast love, O Lord, be upon us,
even as we hope in you.

CALL TO CONFESSION
[spoken from the font]
Even in our faithlessness,
God loves us still
and waits in mercy to forgive.
Trusting in the promises given at our baptism,
let us confess our sin before God and one another.

PRAYER OF CONFESSION
Holy God,   *Gen. 15:5; Heb. 11:1;*
you promise us a life full of blessing,   *Luke 12:34, 40*
but we do not always believe.
You incite us to hope,
but we fall back into fear.
You urge us to give freely,
but we cling to what we have.
You call us to watch at all times for you,
but we grow lazy and self-absorbed.
Forgive us.
Increase our hope, enlarge our hearts,

124

and keep us alert to the wonders you work
in the world every day.
For the sake of Jesus we pray. Amen.

DECLARATION OF FORGIVENESS
[spoken from the font]
Hear the good news!
[Water is poured into the font, visibly and audibly.]
By faith we have been saved,
our guilty hearts washed clean.
Refreshed, revived, and renewed,
empowered by the Holy Spirit,
live as ones who are forgiven and freed,
giving thanks to God.

PRAYER OF THE DAY
God of grace,
who are we that you should care for us?
Yet you surprise us with grace,
infuse us with hope,
and teach us a better way.
Make us ever more faithful,
and ever more grateful,
as we watch for the coming of your Son, Jesus,
in whose name we pray. **Amen.**

PRAYER FOR ILLUMINATION
Holy God,
by your Spirit enlighten us;
illumine us;
inspire us;
not for our sakes,
but for the sake of Jesus Christ,
in whom we live. **Amen.**

PRAYERS OF INTERCESSION
[A period of silence follows each intercession.]
God of blessing,
you fling the stars into the heavens
and show us more blessings than we can count.

You give us treasure that cannot be destroyed.
You promise us a feast and peace without end.
And you hear our prayers.

We pray for your world, wounded and scarred:
  heal earth's body, and lead us to care.

We pray for your church, divided and angry:
  unite us in mission, and grow us in love.

We pray for the lost, the forgotten, the lonely:
  gather them in, and show us how to love.

We pray for the addicted:
  save them and strengthen them.

We pray for those who have no hope:
  give them faith in you.

We pray for the greedy:
  make them generous.

We pray for the poor:
  sustain them and give them hope.

We pray for all those whose burdens we carry in our hearts,
  and offer them up to you:
  heal them, comfort them, guide them, make them whole.

Now increase our faith, and amplify our hope,
  that by the power of your Spirit
  we might serve you well and be ready to greet you
  when Christ comes in glory. **Amen.**

INVITATION TO THE OFFERING
In obedience to Christ
and with love for our neighbors,
let us bring our offerings to God.

PRAYER OF THANKSGIVING/DEDICATION
Generous God,
you pour out blessing and cover us with gifts of love.
Accept these offerings for the sake of your children,
that they may proclaim your mercy and embody your grace.
In Jesus' name we ask it. **Amen.**

CHARGE

Do not be afraid,
for it is the Father's good pleasure to give you the kingdom.

BLESSING

May the blessing of God,
Father, Son, and Holy Spirit,
be with you this day and every day
until Christ comes to make all things well.

Questions for Reflection

What does it mean to "desire a better country . . . a heavenly one" (Heb. 11:16)? How does looking forward to a heavenly home change the way we live on earth?

Household Prayer: Morning

On this new day, Lord,
make me watchful
for all that you are doing in the world;
keep me faithful,
that I may do your will in all things;
and hold me in your grace,
as I seek to do the same for all I meet. Amen.

Household Prayer: Evening

Here at the end of the day, O Lord,
help me to entrust my cares to you.
Grant me grace for my failings
and rest for my weary soul,
that I may be strengthened
to do your will and share your love
when a new day dawns. Amen.

Proper 15

(Sunday between August 14 and August 20 inclusive)

SEMICONTINUOUS

Isaiah 5:1–7   Hebrews 11:29–12:2
Psalm 80:1–2, 8–19   Luke 12:49–56

OPENING WORDS / CALL TO WORSHIP

Since we are surrounded by so great a cloud of witnesses,   *Heb. 12:1*
let us also lay aside every weight
and the sin that clings so closely,
and let us run with perseverance
the race that is set before us.
Mindful of the gifts we receive
and confident of the sustenance the Lord provides,
let us worship God.

CALL TO CONFESSION

Trusting in God's hopes for us,
let us come before God with contrite hearts,
asking for reconciliation and seeking peace.

PRAYER OF CONFESSION

**God of hope, we confess
our disregard of your care . . .
our doubt of your providence . . .
our blindness to signs of your love.
We are afraid to risk our comforts to find new life;
we separate ourselves from you and from others
and foster divisions between those you love.
Help us to amend our lives
and make us your faithful people
who bear the good fruit of your Word in the world.
Through Jesus Christ, our Lord. Amen.**

DECLARATION OF FORGIVENESS

God hears our confession,
rejoicing as we desire amendment of life.
God lifts us from our despondency
to rejoice in the company of the saints.
God acknowledges the forces that separate us,
and brings us to peace.
Rejoice in the knowledge of our reconciliation
and a life lived in the presence of God.

PRAYER OF THE DAY

God of Peace,   *Luke12:49–56*
your call, at times, appears to divide us from
    one another.
Help us to overcome our fears and respond in courage.
Give us faith to trust the unity that is beyond our sight.
Give us your eyes to recognize the signs before us.
We ask this in the confidence of your Son, Jesus Christ
    our Lord. **Amen.**

PRAYER FOR ILLUMINATION

God of Wisdom,   *Luke 12:49–56*
we eagerly seek your presence
in our lives
and in the world.
By your Spirit,
    speak your word to us,
and give us your grace to recognize the abundant signs
    of your care for us,
so that we might be freed to act in the world
with courage and abandon. **Amen.**

PRAYERS OF INTERCESSION

Gathered as your people,
we offer the concerns of our life and the world saying,
God of mercy, hear our prayer.

We pray for the universal church.
May discord among denominations yield to unity

and a common commitment to share the good news of Christ.
God of mercy, **hear our prayer.**

We pray for the world.
Prod us to engage in acts of mission and service
that further the kingdom
and honor the care that God has given us.
God of mercy, **hear our prayer.**

We pray for those who hold authority in government.
Enable policymakers to enact justice,
transforming places of violence and conflict
into havens of respite and peace.
God of mercy, **hear our prayer.**

We pray for all those in our community
who are suffering the burden of illness, distress,
or any kind of pain.
God of mercy, **hear our prayer.**

We remember all those who have died
and joined the great cloud of witnesses in heaven.
God of mercy, **hear our prayer.**

Heavenly Creator,
you inspire us to trust in the things we cannot see
and to ground our faith in your promises to us.
Give us the clarity of your vision,
and make us ready to serve you as we await your return.
We ask this through your Son, Jesus Christ our Lord. **Amen.**

INVITATION TO THE OFFERING
Mindful of the abundance we have received in Christ,
we offer ourselves and our gifts to the world.

PRAYER OF THANKSGIVING/DEDICATION
We trust, O God,   *Isa. 5:1–7*
in your provision and loving kindness.
Use these gifts and our lives
that we might bear your fruit with praise and thanksgiving.
We ask this in the confidence of your mercy and love. **Amen.**

CHARGE

God is present to us,   *Luke 12:49–56*
calling us to attend to our lives
and our world.
Confident in God's provision and direction
we go forth inspired,
seeking reconciliation in places of division,
honoring the plight of those on the margins,
and filled with gratitude for God's promises.

BLESSING

May the God of creation and restoration
give you confidence in the daily tasks set before you.
The God of love and compassion,
assure you of your heritage as a child of God.
The God of guidance and inspiration,
mold you in God's image.

And the blessing of God,
Creator, Redeemer, and Sustainer,
be with you and remain with you always.

Questions for Reflection

How do you reconcile a sense of division within yourself and the world
with the unity we are promised as the people of God? What sustains you
in times of conflict? Identify some occasions in your life when you were
unable to recognize an invitation to reconciliation and wholeness.

Household Prayer: Morning

Lord of Life,
we greet this new day
sustained by the great cloud of witnesses
who praise your name.
Help us to lay aside any burden or distraction
that might prevent us from fully serving you this day.
Give us perseverance and joy
so that we may come to the end of the day
confident in your presence
and aware of your blessings. Amen.

Household Prayer: Evening

God of Hope,
confirm for us at the close of this day
the fulfillment of your promise of provision.
Release our concerns for things done and left undone.
Give us your peace
so that we rise refreshed
to serve you with openness and love. Amen.

Proper 15

(Sunday between August 14 and August 20 inclusive)

COMPLEMENTARY

Jeremiah 23:23–29	Hebrews 11:29–12:2
Psalm 82	Luke 12:49–56

OPENING WORDS / CALL TO WORSHIP
God gives justice to the weak and the orphan;   *Ps. 82:3, 4*
God rescues the weak and the needy.
Blessed be the one, holy and living God,
now and forever.

CALL TO CONFESSION
Let us confess our sins,
for God is gracious and strong to save.

PRAYER OF CONFESSION
God of goodness and truth,   *Jer. 23:25–29*
we have failed to seek after your wisdom
and have followed paths that have led away
    from you.
Forgive our foolish ways,
and lead us in your truth,
that we may live in the fullness of life
as you intend through Christ our Lord. Amen.

DECLARATION OF FORGIVENESS
Beloved, your sins are forgiven,   *Ps. 80:2, 19*
for God is merciful and just.
Therefore, be reconciled to the Lord
and to one another,
walking in the light of Christ.

PRAYER OF THE DAY

Faithful God,
you have blessed us with the
    inheritance of grace
that we might live as people of justice,
    righteousness, and peace.
Stir in us your power and fill us with
    the love of Christ,
strong and true,
that we may be always eager to serve your
    promised reign of peace. **Amen.**

Heb. 11:29–12:2;
Luke 12:49–56

PRAYER FOR ILLUMINATION

Holy God,
your Word is like fire.
By the power of your Spirit,
illumine our sight
and enflame our hearts,
that we may live lives more faithful to your will. **Amen.**

Jer. 23:29

PRAYERS OF INTERCESSION

[A time of silence follows each petition.]
God of mercy,
throughout the ages you have led us
through trial and hardship,
providing all our needs
and speaking words of promise.
Confident of your faithfulness,
we bring to you our prayers for the world.

We pray for the mission of your church,
that it may plant and grow faithful people to serve
    others in love.

We pray for the world,
that all might tend to your justice and watch for
    your coming reign.

We pray for all who suffer,
that our care for them may reveal your healing.

We pray for your creation,
that we may cultivate its flourishing.

We remember before you those who have died
and pray for those who will die today,
that they may rest in light divine.

Through Christ, with Christ,
in the unity of the Holy Spirit,
all glory and honor are yours, almighty Father,
forever and ever. **Amen.**

INVITATION TO THE OFFERING
Our God, who is faithful,
blesses us with an abundance of gifts.
In gratitude, let us offer all that we have
and all that we are for the love of Christ,
the pioneer and perfecter of our faith.

PRAYER OF THANKSGIVING/DEDICATION
God of the ages,   *Heb. 11:29–12:2*
surrounded by a great cloud of witnesses,
we faithfully add our gifts
to those who have gone before us
throughout the generations.
Bless these gifts that they may yield an increase
for the spreading of your love in the world. **Amen.**

CHARGE
Christ walked in perfect faith   *Heb. 11:29–12:2;*
that we might follow in the way   *Luke 12:49–56*
    of peace.
Go in peace to love and serve the Lord.

BLESSING
May Christ, the pioneer and perfecter   *Heb. 11:29–12:2;*
    of our faith,   *Luke 12:49–56*
grant you the perseverance
    and courage
to follow him in all justice, righteousness,
    and peace.

Questions for Reflection

How has following Christ caused conflict in your own life or in the life of someone you know?

Household Prayer: Morning

Laboring God of this new age,
give me wisdom and courage to understand your will
as I live your word this day. Amen.

Household Prayer: Evening

Lord, I have done my best to serve you this day,
yet I often feel I have left so much undone.
Help me to find my rest in you
and trust that in the evening I shall be saved by Love. Amen.

Proper 16

(Sunday between August 21 and August 27 inclusive)

SEMICONTINUOUS

Jeremiah 1:4–10	Hebrews 12:18–29
Psalm 71:1–6	Luke 13:10–17

OPENING WORDS / CALL TO WORSHIP
God is our rock and our fortress,   *Ps. 71:3, 5*
our refuge and strength.
God is our hope and our trust.
Praise the Lord!

CALL TO CONFESSION
Our God is compassionate and merciful,   *Jer. 1:4–10*
knowing us with an intimacy we cannot comprehend.
There is nothing we have done,
or left undone,
that is not already known by God.

This gives us confidence,
to be fully ourselves,
that we can be fully forgiven.

PRAYER OF CONFESSION
God of Life,   *Heb. 12:28, 29; Jer. 1:5;*
you come to us as a consuming fire,   *Luke 13:13*
and the one who has consecrated us before time.

You promise us a kingdom that cannot be shaken
and call us to serve you with praise and thanksgiving.

But we forget,
and yield to fear.

We trust in the tangible rewards of this world,
and neglect your promises.

We confess that we are a divided people;
we foster separations and widen rifts
in our families, our communities, and in the world.

Open us to your healing.
Free us from all that distances us from your presence.
Give us your grace
and inspire us to serve you with courage;
through Jesus Christ who comes to save. Amen.

DECLARATION OF FORGIVENESS

Promising forgiveness and the sustenance we need to
amend our lives,
God rejoices in our longing for wholeness.
Give thanks that we have been known and forgiven,
set free to live the resurrected life of faith.

PRAYER OF THE DAY

God of healing and reconciliation,   *Luke 13:10–17*
you free us from our burdens
and promise us safety and refuge.
Help us to trust in your power,
that we may praise you without qualification
and rejoice in the power of your Son,
Jesus Christ our Lord. **Amen.**

PRAYER FOR ILLUMINATION

Almighty God,   *Jer. 1:4–10;*
you know us better than we know ourselves.   *Luke 13:10–17*
By your word, give us wisdom,
by your Spirit, grant us healing,
and set us free to serve you with love.
We ask this through the One who heals in
your name,
Jesus Christ. **Amen.**

PRAYERS OF INTERCESSION

Let us pray to our sovereign, saying,
God of mercy, hear our prayer.

Almighty God,   *Luke 13:10–17*
you invite us to honor and reverence your name
through acts of praise and thanksgiving.
Hear us as we articulate the concerns of our lives,
    our community, and the world.
God of mercy, **hear our prayer**.

We pray for your holy church.
Make us humble in our service
and generous with our invitations to the outcast.
God of mercy, **hear our prayer.**

We pray for the needs of the world.
Spur leaders to forgo the honor and privileges of power
and to address the concerns of the poor.
God of mercy, **hear our prayer.**

We pray for those in our community
who are burdened by suffering:
the sick, those in need,
and all who seek a deeper knowledge of you.
God of mercy, **hear our prayer.**

We pray for the departed.
We rejoice that they have returned to the place of
    their consecration
and rejoice in the company of the saints.
God of mercy, **hear our prayer.**

God of grace and compassion,
you honor those in our world who do not seek tribute
    or respect.
Help us to expand our vision,
that we might release our need for privilege
and instead seek the honor of your service.
We ask this through the mediation of your Son,
Jesus Christ our Lord. **Amen.**

INVITATION TO THE OFFERING
Mindful of the generosity of God
and the awareness that all we have has been given,
let us respond with the offerings of our lives and labor.

PRAYER OF THANKSGIVING/DEDICATION
Loving God,   *Jer. 1:4–10*
we rejoice that our lives are already consecrated by you.
Inspired by the knowledge of your love,
giving thanks for the gifts you offer us each day,
we pray that these offerings
and our lives
may further your kingdom on earth. **Amen.**

CHARGE
Go forth into the world rejoicing,   *Jer. 1:4–10; Ps. 71:1–6;*
sure of the healing God offers.   *Heb. 12:28*
Share the good news with all,
seeking those who feel unknown and forgotten.
Be strengthened in your faith,
and trust in the kingdom that cannot be shaken.

BLESSING
May the blessing of God,   *Ps. 71:1–6; Heb. 12:29*
like a mother's love, sustain you;
may the peace of God,
like a strong castle, protect you;
may the hope of God,
like a consuming fire, enlighten you,
this day and forevermore.

Questions for Reflection

When are times that you are not open to God's healing? How does the knowledge of God's love and care for you open you more to God's healing? How do you seek God as a refuge in your daily life?

Household Prayer: Morning

God of life and love,
we come to this new day
refreshed from the refuge of sleep and rest.
Sustain us in the coming hours, that we might return this evening,
inspired by your witness in the world
and having done your will. Amen.

Household Prayer: Evening

Lord and keeper of our days,
give us your rest this night.
Release from us the burdens of the day.
Awaken us, refreshed for your service at the dawn,
 upright in our praise and thanksgiving. Amen.

Proper 16

(Sunday between August 21 and August 27 inclusive)

COMPLEMENTARY

Isaiah 58:9b–14   Hebrews 12:18–29
Psalm 103:1–8   Luke 13:10–17

OPENING WORDS / CALL TO WORSHIP
The Lord will guide you continuously   *Isa. 58:11*
and satisfy your needs in parched places;
you shall be like a watered garden,
whose spring never fails.
With thanksgiving and praise,
let us worship God.

CALL TO CONFESSION
The prophet Isaiah assures us   *Isa. 58:9a*
that when we cry for help,
God will answer.
So then, let us confess our sin,
confident that God is ready to forgive.

PRAYER OF CONFESSION
God of justice and love,   *Jer. 58:9–13*
we confess to you and to each other
that we have not offered food to the hungry
or satisfied the needs of the afflicted.
We have spoken evil of others and pointed fingers
     in blame.
We have turned away from you and our community,
pursuing instead our own self-interests.
Parched for mercy, we cry out for your help.
Forgive us, God, and teach us your ways,
that we may be renewed like a garden freshly
     watered. Amen.

DECLARATION OF FORGIVENESS
[Water is poured into the font.]
In the waters of baptism we receive abundant mercy,
flowing like a spring that never runs dry.
Forgiven and freed,
we are reconciled with God and with one another.
The peace of Christ be with you all.
And also with you.
[The people may share a sign of peace.]

PRAYER OF THE DAY
Holy One, we bless you with all that is within us
as we remember your benefits to us.
Open our hearts to helping those most in need,
that our community and nation may be rebuilt
and restored. **Amen.**

Ps. 103:1–2; Isa. 58:12–14

PRAYER FOR ILLUMINATION
God of justice and mercy,
by your Holy Spirit inspire us through your word,
and shape our lives according to your will.
Through Jesus Christ we pray. **Amen.**

PRAYERS OF INTERCESSION
God of wisdom,
you work for vindication and justice for
all who are oppressed,
and you call us to work with you to fulfill
that purpose.
**The Lord says, "I hear your cry for help,
and I am here."**
We pray for the church and for all who work to
bring justice to the oppressed.
**The Lord says, "I hear your cry for help,
and I am here."**
We pray for peace with justice among nations,
religions, and people.
**The Lord says, "I hear your cry for help,
and I am here."**

Ps. 103:6; Isa. 58:9, 12; Luke 1:46; 13:11

We pray for those suffering in places torn by
    war and natural disasters.
The Lord says, "I hear your cry for help,
    and I am here."
We pray for those who are bent over by oppression,
    especially women,
in this nation and around the world.
The Lord says, "I hear your cry for help,
    and I am here."
We pray for those living with long-term illness
    who are longing for relief.
The Lord says, "I hear your cry for help,
    and I am here."
God of Healing Love, through Jesus Christ
    you have come to us and
shown us the way of renewal and restoration.
Empower us now through the meeting of our faith
    and your grace,
that we may do your work in the world and magnify
    your holy name. **Amen.**

INVITATION TO THE OFFERING
Since we are receiving a kingdom that cannot be shaken,   *Heb. 12:28*
let us give thanks,
by which we offer to God an acceptable worship
with reverence and awe.
Offer to God the gifts of your life and labor
and come into God's courts with praise.
[or]
If you offer your food to the hungry   *Isa. 58:10*
and satisfy the needs of the afflicted,
then your light shall rise in the darkness.
Offer to God the gifts of your life and labor
and come into God's courts with praise.

PRAYER OF THANKSGIVING/DEDICATION
Lord of the Sabbath,   *Luke 13:10–17*
we rejoice in offering you these gifts,
that our lives may show forth the wondrous healing
of your love in the world. **Amen**

CHARGE

Go forth in faith,
trusting in the God who heals every infirmity.

BLESSING

May God bless your going out and coming in
from this time forth and forevermore.

Questions for Reflection

The writer of Hebrews says that God is a "consuming fire" (Heb. 12:29).
Why is this good news?

Household Prayer: Morning

Bless the Lord, O my soul,
and all that is within me bless God's holy name.
Bless the Lord, O my soul,
and do not forget all God's benefits. Amen.

Household Prayer: Evening

Healing God, you long to set me free from bondage
so that I may serve you in perfect freedom:
forgive the ways in which I have been unable
to stand in your freedom this day,
and strengthen me this night
that in the morning I may arise
in the support and goodness of your love. Amen.

Proper 17

(Sunday between August 28 and September 3 inclusive)

SEMICONTINUOUS

Jeremiah 2:4–13	Hebrews 13:1–8, 15–16
Psalm 81:1, 10–16	Luke 14:1, 7–14

OPENING WORDS / CALL TO WORSHIP

God calls us to service,   *Heb.13:1–2, 8*
rather than honor.
God call us to love the unknown,
rather than the familiar.
We come to this time of worship,
trusting in the grace of Jesus Christ,
who is the same yesterday, today, and forever.

CALL TO CONFESSION

God invites us to mutual love.   *Heb. 13:1;*
But to find that mutuality, we must release   *Luke 14:1, 7–14*
our need for honor,
our desire for privilege.
In humility let us seek forgiveness,
trusting in the promises of God
in Christ Jesus our Lord.

PRAYER OF CONFESSION

Merciful God, forgive us for we exalt ourselves   *Luke 14:1, 7–14*
and mock the humble.
We choose to believe we are self-sufficient
rather than trust in your strength.

Open us to your spirit,
that we might serve all people
without regard to the outcome,
devoting ourselves to your honor alone.
We pray in Jesus' name. Amen.

DECLARATION OF FORGIVENESS

God rejoices when we repent and return, *Jer. 2:5; Ps. 81:16*
offering us finest wheat
and honey from the rock
to sustain us in new life.
Rejoice! For you have been reconciled
to God and to one another.
With joy, seek the honor of God's service. **Amen.**

PRAYER OF THE DAY

Holy God,
you alone are worthy of honor and praise.
Open our eyes to see the world as you see it.
Give us the wisdom to witness your presence
    in all people.
Transform us in love,
grow us in our faith,
call us to love with a full heart
and to share your promises with all people. **Amen.**

PRAYER FOR ILLUMINATION

God of Wisdom, *Heb. 13:8*
open us to the work of your Spirit,
that we may hear
and faithfully respond
to your holy Word. **Amen.**

PRAYERS OF INTERCESSION

Let us pray to the Lord, saying,
God of mercy, hear our prayer.

Gracious God,
you call us to relinquish the cares and concerns of
    our lives to you,
so that we might serve you in perfect freedom.
Hear us as we bring before you
the petitions of our hearts and minds.
God of mercy, **hear our prayer.**

We offer our prayers for the universal church.
May our words and actions bring honor to your name
and teach us true humility.
God of mercy, **hear our prayer.**

We offer our prayers for the needs of the world.
May peace pervade in all places of conflict and violence.
God of mercy, **hear our prayer.**

We offer our prayers for those who suffer
from sickness of mind, body, or spirit
and all those who care for them.
God of mercy, **hear our prayer.**

We pray for those who have died,
who now worship in the presence of Christ,
and those who will die today.
God of mercy, **hear our prayer.**

Almighty God,
you call us to follow you with faithfulness,
even when it challenges our relationships
and the values of our culture.
Help us to release our fears,
nurture us in your ways,
and sustain us as we seek your peace.
We ask this through your Son,
Jesus Christ our Lord. **Amen.**

INVITATION TO THE OFFERING

God gives us more grace than we can ever earn   *Luke 14:7–14*
and sustains us in ways we cannot imagine.
With a spirit of generosity,
let us freely offer ourselves and our gifts to the world.

PRAYER OF THANKSGIVING/DEDICATION

God of grace,
we give thanks for your faithfulness to us,
we give thanks for your hope in us,
we rejoice in the knowledge of your unending grace.
In the light of your mercy,
and confident in your love,
we dedicate these offerings, and ourselves, to you. **Amen.**

CHARGE

God graces us with abundance and inspires
    us to be generous.   *Heb. 13:2, Luke 14:7–14*

Now, go into the world,
confident in the Lord's provision,
seeking those who are the stranger
and providing for those who cannot repay you. **Amen.**

BLESSING

May the God of mystery take you to
    unexpected places,   *Luke 14:1, 7–14*
may the God of humility teach you to
    serve without pride,
may the God of wisdom inspire your
    work in the kingdom;
and the blessing of God,
Creator, Redeemer, and Sanctifier,
be with you now and always.

Questions for Reflection

How does your experience of the culture prevent you from fully embracing
the call to serve with humility? How can you seek out the stranger in your
community? When have you realized that you were doing God's work, only
after the fact?

Household Prayer: Morning

God, in the freshness of the new day,
help us to retain clarity of vision
so that we might seek the honor of your kingdom
rather than the honor of the world.
Sustain us throughout the day so that we might return
filled by the grace of your spirit. Amen.

Household Prayer: Evening

God of compassion,
help us to release the regrets of the day into your care.
Refresh us in our sleep,
that we may rise in the morning
confident in your love and strengthened in our faith. Amen.

Proper 17

(Sunday between August 28 and September 3 inclusive)

COMPLEMENTARY

Sirach 10:12–18 *or* Proverbs 25:6–7   Hebrews 13:1–8, 15–16
Psalm 112   Luke 14:1, 7–14

OPENING WORDS / CALL TO WORSHIP
Sing aloud to God our strength.   *Ps. 81:1*
Shout for joy to the Lord of Life.
Blessed be the one, holy and living God.
Glory to God forever.

CALL TO CONFESSION
Let us confess our sins to the Lord who is
    our helper.   *Heb. 13:6*

PRAYER OF CONFESSION
Lord, all that we have is a gift from you,   *Heb. 13:2; Luke 14:11;*
yet we do not live lives of gratitude.   *Sir. 10:12–13*
We ignore strangers
and turn away from those in need.
We seek honor for ourselves
and allow pride to take root in us.
Forgive our foolish ways, O God,
and restore us to you,
that we may walk in the way of love. Amen.

DECLARATION OF FORGIVENESS
Beloved, your sins are forgiven,   *Heb. 13:5;*
for God promises to never leave us.   *Ps. 112:7b*
Therefore, be at peace and stand secure
    in the Lord.

PRAYER OF THE DAY

Faithful God,   *Heb. 13:1–8, 15–16;*
in Jesus you show us a way of humility   *Luke 14:1, 7–14*
    and hospitality
with power to transform our world.
Give us the grace to love those things that please you
and the courage to live them to your glory. **Amen.**

PRAYER FOR ILLUMINATION

Holy God, your word is a light in darkness
and a source of blessing.
Pour out your Holy Spirit upon us;
enliven our hearts and minds
as we hear your word for us today;
through Jesus Christ we pray. **Amen.**

PRAYERS OF INTERCESSION

[A time of silence may be kept after each intercession.]
Loving God,   *Jer. 2:4–13; Ps. 81:10–13;*
you call us to turn to you in prayer for   *Heb. 13:1*
    the sake of the world.

We pray for the mission of your church:
may it continue in mutual love to the glory of your name.

We pray for a world in need of your counsel:
guide the nations into paths of justice and peace.

We pray for all who suffer:
may they know the healing power of your presence.

We pray for your creation as it longs for its redemption:
teach us to walk as faithful stewards.

We pray for the dying and those who have died:
may they rest in your eternal glory. **Amen.**

INVITATION TO THE OFFERING

Do not neglect to do good and to share what you have,   *Heb. 13:6*
for such sacrifices are pleasing to God.

PRAYER OF THANKSGIVING/DEDICATION

Faithful God, you bless us in Jesus,   *Heb. 13:8, 15*
who is the same yesterday, today, and tomorrow.
And so we praise you with lips that confess his name
and ask your blessing on these gifts
for the life of the world. **Amen.**

CHARGE

Go in peace to love and serve the Lord.

BLESSING

May the grace of our Lord Jesus Christ,
the love of God,
and the communion of the Holy Spirit
be with you all,
this day and forevermore.

Questions for Reflection

Where do you experience mutual love in your life? Is there someone
you disdain? How might you show love for that person in thought,
word, or deed?

Household Prayer: Morning

Holy God,
if the beginning of sin is pride,
then let me walk in your ways and to your glory this day,
rather than to my own. Amen.

Household Prayer: Evening

Lord, you are my helper;
therefore I will not be afraid,
for you are ever with me. Amen.

Proper 18

(Sunday between September 4 and September 10 inclusive)

SEMICONTINUOUS

Jeremiah 18:1–11	Philemon 1–21
Psalm 139:1–6, 13–18	Luke 14:25–33

OPENING WORDS / CALL TO WORSHIP

"Then God said, 'Let us make humankind
   in our image,   *Gen. 1:26–28*
according to our likeness;
and let them have dominion over the fish
   of the sea,
and over the birds of the air,
and over the cattle,
and over all the wild animals of the earth,
and over every creeping thing that creeps
   upon the earth.'

So God created humankind in his image,
in the image of God he created them;
male and female he created them.
God blessed them, and God said to them,
'Be fruitful and multiply,
and fill the earth and subdue it;
and have dominion over the fish of the sea
and over the birds of the air
and over every living thing that moves upon
   the earth.'"

As those who bear the likeness and blessing of God,
as mortals charged with holy purpose,
let us worship the One who summons us to life.

CALL TO CONFESSION

[spoken from the font]
Trusting in the power of God
not only to fashion the world,
but to mend and refashion our hearts,
let us say how it is with us.

PRAYER OF CONFESSION

Holy God,
like children long indulged,
we are quick to presume your pardon,
   your sanction of the way we live.
We turn away from neighbors in need,
   sharing fragments that remain
   only after our cravings have been met.

Merciful Maker,
you created us for better use; remake us now.   *Jer. 18:6*
Where we are distorted
   re-center and reshape us,
   bring us low and raise us up.
Then fire our hearts
   until we shine with your glory
   and find our place in your purpose.
[silent prayer]

DECLARATION OF FORGIVENESS

Hear the sound of love poured out: *2 Cor. 5:17*
[Water is poured into the font.]
If anyone is in Christ, there is a new creation;
   everything old has passed away;
see, everything has become new.
Sisters and brothers,
in the name of the Christ I declare
that your story is known,
   your sin is forgiven,
   your life is made new.
Let us live as those reborn.

PRAYER OF THE DAY

Weaver of life, framer of the ages,   *Gen. 1:26–28; Ps. 139:13,*
we marvel at your artistry and the trust   *15; Col. 1:15*
   you place in us.
From our first cries to our final breaths,
   we are your own.
Bind us now to each other in ways beyond
   our choosing,
that your purpose might find fulfillment in our
   common life and service,
for we pray in the name of Jesus, the firstborn of all creation.
Amen.

PRAYER FOR ILLUMINATION

Holy and merciful God,   *Jer. 18:7, 9, 11; Luke 14:27*
we have come to hear your word.
Help us to bear it.
Break down in us all that resists your will
and plant in us a willingness to turn,
for we would live; we would be your disciples.
By your Spirit, come to us, now,
in ancient texts, in everyday visions, in the need
   of our neighbor;
we pray in the name of Jesus, our light. **Amen.**

PRAYERS OF INTERCESSION

Gracious Creator,
we thank you that you give us to each other,
for we discover new dimensions of your grace
in the friction and comfort of life together.
In your body we learn what it means to be whole.

In your mercy, help us to set our fear aside.
Loosen our grip on what we know,
if it is keeping us from what you would teach us.

We pray for this community and for your church
   all over the world.
You shaped us for service;

show us the good we may do—
for when you use us,
we come alive.

We pray for those we have labeled useless:
for those whose youth and strength are gone,
for those whose convictions are strange to us,
for those who cannot find a place in the economies we trust.

And we pray for those whose prophetic lives challenge and inspire us;
sustain such faithful witnesses.

Lord, we do not know how to pray
for peace in broken lands,
for justice when the weak have no advocate,
for life in the midst of despair;
yet you are the God of Easter, the God of impossible life.
Move in stubborn hearts and settled minds,
give us courage beyond our imagining,
that we might follow where you would lead.

We pray in the name of Jesus,
whose words still burn in our hearts,
whose breath still unsettles your people. **Amen.**

INVITATION TO THE OFFERING
All that we are points back to our Creator;
all that we have is gift and trust.
God will finish what God has begun;
we have the privilege of taking part.

With grateful hearts,
let us bring our tithes and offerings
to the God from whom they came.

PRAYER OF THANKSGIVING/DEDICATION
God of all creation,   *Luke 14:26–27*
your claim on us is total;
your desire for us, complete.
We cannot follow Christ from a comfortable distance.

Yet we ask that you would receive us this day
and use what we bring.
Keep sending your Spirit into our hearts,
until we yield all that we love
and all that we fear
to your holy purpose.
For we long to cede our lives to you;
we long to know the fullness of your joy.
We dare to pray in the name of Jesus,
who gave his life out of love for the world.
Amen.

CHARGE

Paul wrote to Philemon,   *Phlm. 6*
"I pray that the sharing of your faith may become effective
when you perceive all the good we may do for Christ."

BLESSING

May the Artist who crafted you continue to shape   *Ps. 139:13;*
  your heart,   *Matt. 28:19-20*
may the Christ who commissioned you, charge you
  with purpose,   *Luke 14:27*
may the Spirit that stirs you, help you to carry
  the cross,
that you may honor your Creator and bless
  the world.

Questions for Reflection

Where have you seen relationships redefined by faith? Who have you
come to claim as a family member, against all odds? Who do you still
label "useless"? What would it take for you to see that person as a sister or
brother?

Household Prayer: Morning

God of all creation,
you made the hands that stirred unthinking at the start of this day.
As the hours slip by, help me to be more mindful of the good they
  might do:

in the greetings they might offer,
in the burdens they might bear,
in the worry they might soothe.

Prompt me to keep them open—
not clinging to what you have entrusted
but freely offering, freely receiving,
in response to this day's needs.

May each small motion be a sign of trust,
a reminder that my life is in your hands. Amen.

Household Prayer: Evening

God of every beginning, every ending,
as I remember the faces I saw this day,
    in moments ordinary and extraordinary—
as I recall reports of hardship far away—
help me to recognize family forgotten by my heart,
    sisters and brothers entrusted to me.

As I rest this night in your care,
mend my courage and fire my imagination,
that I might be truly useful to you.
Plant me where you need me, in the name of the Christ. Amen.

Proper 18

(Sunday between September 4 and September 10 inclusive)

COMPLEMENTARY

Deuteronomy 30:15–20   Philemon 1–21
Psalm 1   Luke 14:25–33

OPENING WORDS / CALL TO WORSHIP
Happy are those who delight in the Word of God.   *Ps. 1:1–3*
They are like trees planted by streams of water,
and they will flourish.

CALL TO CONFESSION
In penitence and in faith,
let us confess our sin to the One
who waits to pour out mercy upon us.

PRAYER OF CONFESSION
Holy God,
we confess that we fail to put our trust in you completely.
Instead, we calculate our gains and losses,
hoarding the things that do not lead to abundant life.
Forgive us,
and help us to treasure only you,
that we may follow you faithfully
and discover the blessings only you can give. Amen.

DECLARATION OF FORGIVENESS
Beloved, your sins are forgiven.   *Ps. 1*
Therefore be at peace to follow the good road,
for the Lord watches over the way of the righteous.

PRAYER OF THE DAY
Extravagant God,
you pour out blessings upon us

and lead us on the path of true life.
Help us to choose your way again and again,
that we might revel in your love
and reflect it to all we meet.
In the name of Jesus we pray. **Amen.**

PRAYER FOR ILLUMINATION

God of wisdom,
by your Spirit speak this day a word of life,
and plant in us the power of your righteous love;
through Jesus Christ, our Lord. **Amen.**

PRAYERS OF INTERCESSION

Loving God, we offer our prayers this day   *Jer. 18:7–11;*
in gratitude and thanksgiving,   *Ps. 139:1–6, 13–18;*
for in Christ you have laid a foundation for us   *Phlm. 1–21;*
that we might follow you more closely.   *Luke 14:25–33*

We pray for the mission of your church
and thank you for the joy and encouragement
we receive from you through our church family:
give us the grace to plant faith and build love
wherever you lead us to the benefit of your reign.

We pray for all leaders and people of this world:
give us a clear vision of the world as you intend
and the will to realize that dream of justice and peace for all.

We pray for all who suffer in body, mind, or spirit:
bring refreshment to their hearts through Christ
that they may know your abiding presence
and power to comfort and heal.

We pray for your creation:
convict us of the ways in which we break down and destroy
the fabric of your world
and give us the will to amend our ways
as we seek to live in harmony
    with the goodness you have created.

We pray for the dying and those who have died:
may they rest in your eternal glory with all the saints in light.

Now to you be all the glory,
Father, Son, and Holy Spirit,
now and forever. **Amen.**

INVITATION TO THE OFFERING
Jesus says if we would learn from him,   *Ps. 139; Phlm. 1–6;*
we must follow him.   *Luke 14:25–30, 33*
Large crowds listened to Jesus,
but they turned away when they realized the cost.

Jesus said, "None of you can become my disciple
if you do not give up all of your possessions."
Therefore, be generous with the fruit of your life and labor
on behalf of the good we are called to do for Christ.

PRAYER OF THANKSGIVING/DEDICATION
We give you thanks this day for the goodness and love   *Phlm. 1–22*
that you have shown to us in Christ
and pray your blessing upon these gifts:
may they build your love in the world,
to the honor of your name. **Amen.**

CHARGE
Go in peace to love and serve the Lord.

BLESSING
May the Father, the Son, and the Holy Spirit,
one God, Mother of us all,
keep you in love,
challenge you in faith,
and sustain you with grace,
this day and always.

Question for Reflection

What must you give up to follow Christ more faithfully?

Household Prayer: Morning

Abiding God,
awaken my heart to greet you
and open my lips to sing your praise.
May I follow the way of Christ
ever more fully this day. Amen.

Household Prayer: Evening

Lord, you know my strengths and weaknesses
and how I long to serve you.
Thank you for the love and guidance
you have shown for me this day.
In your book of life are written all my days;
in you I fully trust.
Bless me as I sleep this night
and bring me to tomorrow,
rejoicing in the gift of living ever close to you. Amen.

Proper 19

(Sunday between September 11 and September 17 inclusive)

SEMICONTINUOUS

Jeremiah 4:11–12, 22–28   1 Timothy 1:12–17
Psalm 14   Luke 15:1–10

OPENING WORDS / CALL TO WORSHIP
Let us bow before our Creator,
whose Spirit moves over desert and sea,   *Jer. 4:11–12*
whose Word has the power to create, to judge,
   and to save.
Come, let us worship God.
[or]
The Lord looks down from heaven   *Ps. 14*
to see if there are any who are wise,
who seek after God.
They have all gone astray,
there is no one who is good,
no, not one.
Have they no knowledge,
those who devour God's people
and do not call upon the Lord?
O that our deliverer would come!
Lord, restore our lives
and make us glad.

CALL TO CONFESSION
Sisters and brothers,
there is joy in the presence of the angels of God   *Luke 15:10*
every time we turn toward our home and remember
   whose we are.
With open hearts, let us pray.

PRAYER OF CONFESSION

Creator of the universe,   *Jer. 4:12, 22; Ps. 14:1;*
we imagine that we are in familiar territory,   *Luke 15:5*
    that we know what to expect of this hour,
    that we will leave much the way that we came.
Do not abandon us to our foolishness.

In judgment, illumine our darkness.
In mercy, bear us home—
until we recognize your presence wherever
    evil is confronted,
    truth is spoken,
    and life is restored.
[silent confession]

DECLARATION OF FORGIVENESS

[Water is poured into the font.]
But this we call to mind, and therefore have hope: *Lam. 3:21–24*
The steadfast love of the Lord never ceases,
God's mercies never come to an end;
they are new every morning.
In the name of the Lord,
who is our portion and our hope,
I declare that our sin is forgiven.
May our mouths be filled with praise.

PRAYER OF THE DAY

Gracious God,
when our spirits lift at the beauty of the day,
    you are Lord;
and when chaos threatens to overwhelm
    and we dread the next news cycle—
    still, you are Lord.
Always you are creating, redeeming, sustaining.

Speak then your mercy into this place
until we discover the courage to
open our eyes,
unclench our hands,

and move toward our neighbor in need,
until all the world rises and moves with the rhythm of your grace;
for we long to honor the name of Jesus, by whose breath we pray.
Amen.

PRAYER FOR ILLUMINATION

Mighty God,
you spoke the world into being; speak now to our hearts.   *Gen. 1*
By the power of your Spirit, make these ancient words live,
that we might be shaped into your people,
eager to bear your claim in the world
and to give flesh to your future.
For we pray in the name of Jesus, who leads us into life. **Amen.**

PRAYERS OF INTERCESSION

Spirit of Life,
in the beginning you hovered over creation;
      still you brood over the world.   *Gen. 1:2*
We pray for the earth that mourns: *Jer. 4:28*
for rivers smeared with waste and ground stripped
      and ravaged.
Do not let us wait too long; do not let us
      know disaster.
Teach us, who are foolish, what it means
      to do good. *[silence]*   *Jer. 4:23*

We pray for your scattered children: *Luke 15*
      for . . . *[Add current petitions here.]*,
for the people of *[Haiti, Congo, or another troubled
      but forgotten region]*
whose heartbreak is old news, whose loss is relentless.

We pray for all who cannot rest in safety,
who must remain alert to signs of danger
because their countries are riven by war
or because their homes are torn by violence
or because they have no shelter but the street. *[silence]*
Help us to move with compassion toward those who are in need.

We pray for neighbors who are troubled in mind or body or spirit:
for mothers who face hard illness,
for brothers haunted by anxious thoughts,
for children who do not know whom they can trust.
In the silence of this room we lift the names and faces
    we know into the light of your love:
[silence]
Search them out; bring them home.   *Luke 15:5–6*

God of holy love, of power and truth,
help us neither to bow to fear, nor to be silenced by chaos.
Instead, move us resolutely toward your world in need;
until we share the mercy we have discovered in your name.

We thank you for each sign of your stirring:
for the songs of children,
the lingering sunlight,
the knitting of shattered bones. . . .
[Additional thanksgivings could be inserted here.]
You are present in each reminder of life's grace.

Patient and persistent God, let that grace and
    mercy overflow from our lives   *1 Tim. 1:14–17*
    that we might honor your name in the world;
for we pray in the name of Jesus, who came to seek and
    save what was lost. **Amen.**

INVITATION TO THE OFFERING

Time and again, God clears a path for us   *Ps. 14:2, 6; Jer. 4:22;*
to seek the way of life,   *Luke 15:10*
to do good,
to become a refuge for the poor.
That path lies before us.
With joy, let us offer our gifts and our lives in trust.

PRAYER OF THANKSGIVING/DEDICATION

Holy One,
receive these offerings as you receive our lives.
Gather our false starts and uncertain efforts,
our generosity and our reluctance.

Enliven us with your breath and make your purposes known
that our lives might show forth your glory.
For we pray in the name of Jesus and by the power of your Spirit.
Amen.

CHARGE

Sisters and brothers, we have a choice.
We can stand on the margins of the feast,
    grumbling about the other guests, *Luke 15:2*
or we can join in the dance of seeking and
    saving, feeding and being fed.

BLESSING

May the Creator's holiness burn away our
    complacency, *Jer. 4:11*
may the Living Word expose our foolishness, *Ps. 14:1; John 1:3–5*
may the Spirit of mercy turn us home, *Luke 15*
that God's grace might spill from our lives, giving
    hope to a perishing world. *1 Tim. 1:14–15*

Questions for Reflection

How are you a lost sheep, in need of someone to come and search for
you? How are you a religious leader, grumbling at the community's
disintegrating standards? How are you called to engage in the search for
others who live in isolation from God and community?

Household Prayer: Morning

Persistent God,
as the day begins and the light increases,
let me drink deeply of your grace.
As the day unfolds, when my heart strays from you,
call me back to this moment.
Come after me as surely as a woman searches for treasure lost.

If I am deaf and satisfied,
if I resent the needs of others,
blow strong against me.

Do not leave me in my foolishness—
for I would have your mercy flow from me:
I would be a refuge for those who wander;
I would lend my heart to celebrations;
I would speak your name. Amen.

Household Prayer: Evening

Patient, persistent God,
I offer the day-that-has-been to you,
knowing that I was not alone,
even when I wandered and filled my heart with noise.
[silent prayer]

As darkness falls,
as I yield to sleep,
seek me again in my dreams.
Call to me in ways beyond my knowing
that I might find the strength to feed your people,
that I might live, again, to call your name,
that I might know the joy of every stranger headed home.

For the mercy of the Christ will sustain me
and the power of the Spirit send me forth. Amen.

Proper 19

(Sunday between September 11 and September 17 inclusive)

COMPLEMENTARY

Exodus 32:7–14	1 Timothy 1:12–17
Psalm 51:1–10	Luke 15:1–10

OPENING WORDS / CALL TO WORSHIP

Rejoice with me, people of God.   *Luke 15*
God has gathered us in from the wilderness.
Rejoice with me, people of God.
God has swept away the darkness of the night.
Rejoice with me, people of God.
Today, there is joy in the presence of the angels.

CALL TO CONFESSION

[spoken from the font]
The grace of our Lord overflows for us   *1 Tim. 1:12–17*
through the faith and love that are ours
in Christ Jesus.
Trusting in God's grace, let us confess our sin, saying,
Create in us a clean heart, O God;
put a new and right spirit within us.

PRAYER OF CONFESSION

O Lord, forgive your foolish people.   *Jer. 4:22*
We are skilled in doing evil,
but we do not know how to do good.

Create in us a clean heart, O God;   *Ps. 51:10*
put a new and right spirit within us.

In the folly of our hearts   *Ps. 14:1*
we live as though there is no God.

169

Create in us a clean heart, O God;
put a new and right spirit within us.

We forget all you have done for us,   *Exod. 32:8*
and make false idols to be our gods.

Create in us a clean heart, O God;
put a new and right spirit within us.

We act faithlessly, violently,   *1 Tim. 1:13*
and scorn your name.

Create in us a clean heart, O God;
put a new and right spirit within us.
[silent prayer]

DECLARATION OF FORGIVENESS
The saying is sure and worthy of full acceptance,   *1 Tim. 1:12–27*
that Christ Jesus came into the world to
  save sinners.

Hear the good news!
In Jesus Christ we are forgiven.
Thanks be to God.

PRAYER OF THE DAY
Merciful Lord, in Christ we see   *Luke 15*
the lengths and depths to which you go
  to save us.
Make us glad in our salvation,
so that we may share this good news
with friends and neighbors
and with all the world;
through Jesus Christ our Lord. **Amen.**

PRAYER FOR ILLUMINATION
Holy God, by the gift of your Spirit   *Ps. 51:1–10*
show us the truth that you desire
and teach us wisdom in our hearts.

Let us hear with joy and gladness
the Word that you speak today;
through Jesus Christ our Savior. **Amen.**

PRAYERS OF INTERCESSION

[optional response to each intercession:]
Have mercy, O God,   *Ps. 51:1*
according to your steadfast love.

God of grace, hear our prayers
for your church, your world,
and all those whom we love.

We pray for those who face disaster: *Jer. 4; Exod. 32*
deliver them from evil by your mighty hand.

We pray for those who are lost or lonely: *Luke 15*
seek them out and bring them home to safety.

We pray for those who suffer persecution and violence: *1 Tim. 1*
help them and heal them.

We pray for those who are poor and hungry: *Luke 15*
provide for them by your generous Spirit.

We pray for those who cannot believe: *Ps. 14*
be their refuge and show them your grace.

According to your abundant mercy,
receive all these prayers
and accomplish your purpose in us;
through Jesus Christ our Lord. **Amen.**

INVITATION TO THE OFFERING

As a shepherd searches for a lost sheep,   *Luke 15:1–10*
as a woman searches for a lost coin,
God seeks us out to save us.
With gratitude and joy,
let us offer our lives to the Lord.

PRAYER OF THANKSGIVING/DEDICATION

We rejoice and give you thanks, O God,   *Luke 15:1–10*
for the lost have been found,
sinners have received mercy,
and the dead have been restored to life.
Send us out in your service
to tend your sheep
and show the riches of your grace;
through Jesus Christ our Lord. Amen.

CHARGE

Go now in the strength of the Lord Jesus Christ,   *1 Tim. 1:12–17*
who appoints us for service
and makes us faithful.

BLESSING

May the Ruler of the ages,   *1 Tim. 1:12–17*
the immortal and invisible one,
go with you,
this day and every day.

Questions for Reflection

In Luke 15:1–10, Jesus tells the parable of a shepherd who seeks out
one lost sheep and a woman who searches her home for a missing coin. Is
there someone from whom you are estranged, a distant friend or family
member, or a person from your church you haven't seen in a while? If
appropriate, find a way to contact that person and let them know you have
missed them.

Household Prayer: Morning

O Lord, have mercy on us this day
according to your steadfast love.
Create clean hearts and new spirits within us
and open our lips to declare your praise;
through Jesus Christ our Savior. Amen.

Household Prayer: Evening

Tonight, O God, we give you thanks
for your grace overflowing in our lives
and for the gifts of faith and love in Christ.
Strengthen us for your service,
be patient with us in our failings,
and continue to pour out your mercy upon us;
through Jesus Christ our Lord. Amen.

[or]

We give you thanks and praise, O God,
for seeking us when we were lost,
for sweeping us up from the darkness,
for gathering us into your fold,
and for holding us in the palm of your hand.
Bring all your wandering children home,
so that there may be rejoicing in your church
and joy in the presence of your angels;
through Jesus Christ our Savior. Amen.

Proper 20

(Sunday between September 18 and September 24 inclusive)

SEMICONTINUOUS

Jeremiah 8:18–9:1	1 Timothy 2:1–7
Psalm 79:1–9	Luke 16:1–13

OPENING WORDS / CALL TO WORSHIP
Our help is in the name of the Lord,   *Ps. 79:9; 124:8*
who made heaven and earth.
Help us, O God of our salvation,
    for the glory of your name;
deliver us, and forgive our sins,
    for your name's sake.

CALL TO CONFESSION
[spoken from the font)
If we say that we have no sin,   *1 John 1:8–9*
we deceive ourselves,
and the truth is not in us.
But if we confess our sin,
God who is faithful, washes us clean.
With one heart and voice, let us pray.

PRAYER OF CONFESSION
Creator of the universe,
    casualty of our sin,
      breath of life,   *Ps. 79:9; Jer. 2;*
we come trembling before you   *Luke 16*
for we have hoarded and bartered
    what has never been ours
in the hope of securing our future.
We have yearned for wealth more than we have
    yearned for you.
We have squandered your trust
    and grieved your heart with our betrayal.

Help us, O God of our salvation, for the glory of your name;
deliver us, and forgive our sins, for your name's sake. Amen.

[silent confession]

DECLARATION OF FORGIVENESS

Beloved of God,
the mercy of the Lord is from everlasting
  to everlasting.

Ps. 103:17;
Rom. 8:38–39

It cannot be contained, but must be poured out.
[Water is poured into the font.]
Nothing you have done, nothing you will ever do
is enough to separate you from the love of God
made known in Jesus Christ.
I declare in the name of the risen Christ
that our sin is forgiven and our lives are made new.

PRAYER OF THE DAY

You hear the cries of your people
for justice and mercy;
you answer our prayers
with the gift of your Son,
who bears our burdens
and sets us free.
Speak your truth to us;
purge and refine us;
that we may love and serve you alone. **Amen.**

PRAYER FOR ILLUMINATION

God of life,
by the power of your Spirit come to us now.
Plow our hearts with your living Word
  until we who are broken become fertile with your love,
  for we long to bear fruit in a world that is wasting.
We pray in the name of Jesus, whose charge we bear. **Amen.**

PRAYERS OF INTERCESSION

Holy One,
you are beyond our imagining, beyond our control, beyond
  our comfort.
You will not be bound by our schemes.

Even so we maintain appearances, and we jockey with our neighbors,
even as we make idols from our fears.
But your ways are not our ways.
You are not a god of tidy balance sheets or weekly appointments;
your love is too deep, your claim too pervasive.
You are there when tempers fray and anger erupts.
You are there when anxiety overwhelms and we withdraw.
You are *here* in every bruised heart, every calloused hand, every
    tangled dream.
Move among us now.
Receive our broken spirits as the offerings we bring this day.
Merciful God, breathe deeply into this room your reconciling love,
    your holy expectation.
Allow us now to see the faces of those we have harmed,
    those we have kept at a distance. . . . *[silence]*
Work in us, Lord, until our hearts are softened
    and we dare to seek our neighbor's good.
Teach us to pray with our hands and our feet and our voices.

We lift to you now all that seems irreconcilable in our families,
    in our schools and workplaces . . . *[silence]*
in our nation . . . *[silence]*
in your church . . . *[silence]*
in your world. . . . *[silence]*

We pray for those we identify as leaders in every sphere of life. . . .
    [silence]
We pray for our president, and for all whose decisions
    weigh heavily on others. . . . *[silence]*
Even so, Lord, give us the courage to name ourselves
    as those whose responsibility is great.
Teach us to tend the world you love:
to sow more than we reap,
to heal more than we wound,
to make room for others as you made room for us.

We pray with hearts both eager and reluctant,
trusting that you will meet us—and call to us—
just where we are, in the name of the Christ. **Amen.**

INVITATION TO THE OFFERING

God longs for us to bring everything that we are,
everything that we have,
to this relationship;
God loves us that much.
May the offerings we bring this day be tokens of our reciprocal desire.

PRAYER OF THANKSGIVING/DEDICATION

Gracious God,
source of our daily bread and Sabbath trust,
you feed us with your love
and equip us to share in your purpose.
Receive the offerings of our wounded spirits,
our guarded purses,
our meager strength,
and continue to expand our hearts,
until we live with the boldness and joy of Easter morning;
for we pray in the name of your son, Jesus,
and by the power of your Spirit. **Amen.**

CHARGE AND BLESSING

Sisters and brothers,
however dark the night gets—whatever you have squandered—
know that you are held by a love like this:
the Creator who made you still claims you in covenant love;
the Redeemer who died for your sake, lives again by the Word of God;
the Sustainer of all creation, yet breathes courage into your heart.
Go, then, and serve boldly,
for God's desire encompasses the whole of creation.

Question for Reflection

How do we, individually and corporately, embody both lament for the
world and the hope that is in Christ?

Household Prayer: Morning

In this moment of stillness
before I dress in the claims of the day,
let me stand bare before you
with questions unanswered. . . .

Fill the silence with your nearness,
that I may hear you speak your word
and live this day for you. Amen.

Household Prayer: Evening

Source of my life,
this day I was not promised
now is ending.
I thank you for the grace it was,
noticed and unnoticed.

I lay before you all that I saw.
[Let your day replay in memory.]
I trust to you all that I failed to see.
[Let God bring to mind whatever God might.]

In the gift of the gathering darkness
brood over your creation again,
and restore your image in me,
that I might bear both your grief and your joy in the world;
for I pray in the name of Jesus, whose service was love. Amen.

Proper 20

(Sunday between September 18 and September 24 inclusive)

COMPLEMENTARY

Amos 8:4–7	1 Timothy 2:1–7
Psalm 113	Luke 16:1–13

OPENING WORDS / CALL TO WORSHIP

Praise the Lord, O servants of the Lord! *Ps. 113:1–3*
Blessed be the name of the Lord
from this time on and forevermore.
From the rising of the sun to its setting
the name of the Lord is to be praised.
Blessed be the name of the Lord
from this time on and forevermore.

[or]

Who is like the Lord our God, *Ps. 113*
high above the heavens in glory?
Blessed be the name of the Lord.
Who raises the poor from the dust
and lifts up the needy from the ashes?
Blessed be the name of the Lord.
Who makes light shine in darkness,
gives joy in sorrow,
and brings life out of death?
Blessed be the name of the Lord.

CALL TO CONFESSION

Even though we continually turn away from God,
the Lord is eager to forgive.
Trusting in the promise of grace,
let us confess our sin.

PRAYER OF CONFESSION

Gracious God, you know our sin: *Luke 16; Ps. 79:9*
We have squandered the gifts you have given us.
We have failed to forgive our debtors
as you have forgiven us.
We have been unfaithful and dishonest
in small things and great things alike.
We are shrewd in seeking wealth
and foolish in following your way.

Forgive our sins, O Lord,
for your name's sake.
Make us faithful stewards
of the grace you have given
and generous in forgiving others;
through Jesus Christ our Lord. Amen.

DECLARATION OF FORGIVENESS

Our loving God desires everyone to be saved   *1 Tim. 2:4*
and to come to the knowledge of the truth.
Hear the good news!
In Jesus Christ we are forgiven.
Thanks be to God.

PRAYER OF THE DAY

Faithful God, we give you thanks   *Luke 16*
that in Jesus Christ you have entrusted us
with the richness of your glory
and the treasure of your grace.
Make us faithful stewards of your good gifts,
that we may show your love to this generation
and welcome us into your eternal home,
where we will worship and serve you forever;
through Christ our Savior. **Amen.**

PRAYER FOR ILLUMINATION

God our Savior, as we hear your Word   *1 Tim. 2*
send your Holy Spirit

to be our teacher of faith and truth
and show us how we are called to live;
through Jesus Christ our Lord. **Amen.**

PRAYERS OF INTERCESSION

[optional response to each intercession:]
Help us, O God of our salvation;   *Ps. 79:9*
deliver us for the glory of your name.

You are one, O God,   *1 Tim. 2*
and you have given us one mediator:
Christ Jesus our Lord;
it is in his name that we offer our prayers
of thanksgiving, intercession, and supplication.

For the poor and needy in our land,   *Amos 8*
and in every land,
those who are trampled on by the rich,
bought and sold for profit . . . . *[silent prayer]*

For families torn apart by violence,   *Ps. 79*
lands laid waste by destruction,
and cities ruined by war . . . . *[silent prayer]*

For all those who are beset by illness or grief,   *Jer. 8–9*
whose hearts are sick,
whose joy is gone . . . . *[silent prayer]*

We pray these things through Jesus Christ   *1 Tim. 2*
who gave himself a ransom for all. **Amen.**

INVITATION TO THE OFFERING

Jesus teaches us that no one can serve two masters.   *Luke 16*
We cannot serve both God and wealth.
Let us entrust our treasure to the Lord
who has provided so abundantly for us
with generosity and grace beyond measure.

PRAYER OF THANKSGIVING/DEDICATION

Who is like you, O Lord our God?   *Ps. 113*
You look with mercy upon the earth;
you lift up the poor from the dust
and give them a place at your table.
Teach us to sing your praise forever
and to show your love to those in need;
through Jesus Christ our Savior. **Amen.**

CHARGE AND BLESSING

Lead a life of peacefulness,   *1 Tim. 2*
of godliness and dignity,
seeking what is good and acceptable and right
in the sight of God our Savior.
May the God of hope sustain you,
the Holy Spirit keep you,
and Christ the Lord walk with you,
today and every day.

Questions for Reflection

First Timothy 2:1–7 includes some important instructions on prayer: "I urge that supplications, prayers, intercessions, and thanksgivings be made for everyone" (1 Tim. 2:1). In particular, the writer encourages us to pray for "kings and all who are in high positions" (2:2). In your own practice of prayer, how do you remember leaders and others in positions of authority in your nation or community? What kind of prayers do you think they need?

Household Prayer: Morning

We praise and worship you, O God.
From the heights of the heavens
you look down upon the earth
to lift up the poor and needy.
Help us to glorify your name this day,
from the rising of the sun to its setting;
through Jesus Christ our Lord. Amen.

Household Prayer: Evening

We belong to you, O God;
we are yours alone.
Keep us faithful as you are faithful—
in all things, great and small—
so that when this world passes away
we may be welcomed into an eternal home;
through Jesus Christ our Savior. Amen.

Proper 21

(Sunday between September 25 and October 1 inclusive)

SEMICONTINUOUS

Jeremiah 32:1–3a, 6–15   1 Timothy 6:6–19
Psalm 91:1–6, 14–16   Luke 16:19–31

OPENING WORDS / CALL TO WORSHIP

When they call to me, I will answer them,   *Ps. 91:15*
   says the Lord.
I will be with them in trouble,
I will rescue and honor them.
With thanksgiving and praise, let us worship God.

CALL TO CONFESSION

Trusting in the mercy of God,   *Luke 16*
let us confess our sins,
that grace might bridge,
and we might cross,
the great chasm between us.

PRAYER OF CONFESSION

Dressed in fine linen,   *Luke 16*
we feast sumptuously every day,
  while others long
  to satisfy their hunger.
We have Moses and the prophets,
yet we remain
  unconvinced,
  waiting for some human warning.
Forgive us.
In your mercy,
  convince and comfort us,
  and lead us to righteousness
  through Jesus Christ, our Savior. Amen.

DECLARATION OF FORGIVENESS

Through Christ we are   *Luke 16*
carried away by the angels,
comforted by Father Abraham,
our hunger—satisfied,
our agony—cooled,
and our sins—forgiven.

Believe the good news:
in Jesus Christ we are forgiven.

PRAYER OF THE DAY

Eternal God,
help us to measure our time,
in faithful generosity,
that your will be done,
your kingdom come,
for life everlasting,
in Jesus Christ our Lord. **Amen.**

PRAYER FOR ILLUMINATION

God of the Prophets,   *Jer. 32*
by the power of the Holy Spirit
speak your Word to us,
and seal it within us,
that we may heed your call. **Amen.**

PRAYERS OF INTERCESSION

*[Calls and responses may be spoken between a leader and
the assembly or between two halves of the assembly.]*
Lord,   *Ps. 91*
we call to you,
our refuge,
provide your safe space.
We call to you,
our fortress,
provide your strength.
We call to you,
our trust,
provide your vision.

We call to you,
our deliverer,
provide your promise.
We call to you,
our cover,
provide your gentleness.
We call to you,
our faithful,
provide your presence.
We call to you,
our shield,
provide your defense.
We call to you,
our bunker,
provide your confidence.
We call to you,
our protector,
provide your future.
We call to you,
our rescuer,
provide your breath.
We call to you,
our satisfaction,
provide your peace.
We call to you,
our savior,
provide your grace. **Amen.**

INVITATION TO THE OFFERING

We brought nothing   *1 Tim. 6*
into the world,
so that we can take nothing
out of the world.

Let us give
both the gifts we have been given
and our truest selves
with glad and generous hearts.

PRAYER OF THANKSGIVING/DEDICATION

God who gives life   *1 Tim. 6*
to all things,
and richly provides us
with everything,
use these,
our offerings,
to take hold of,
and show us,
the life that really is. Amen.

CHARGE

Fight the good fight of faith,   *1 Tim. 6*
take hold of the eternal life
    to which you were called,
take hold of the life that really is.

BLESSING

Leave in jubilee,   *Jer. 32*
knowing,
somewhere,
in an earthen jar,
is the deed to the land of the Lord,
    a land of houses and fields and vineyards,
    a land of redemption,
    a land that shall be bought again.

Questions for Reflection

Like the prophet Amos, Jesus has harsh words for those who live in luxury
and ignore the needs of the poor. The epistle reading warns that "the love
of money is a root of all kinds of evil" (1 Tim. 6:10). What is an appropriate
Christian attitude toward wealth? How are we called to treat those who are
poor?

Household Prayer: Morning

My God,
out of the darkness

that stalks the night
   you bring the light of morning.
Let my love for you
   not waste at noonday,
    but burn until evening again. Amen.

Household Prayer: Evening

My God, Most High,
   day is done.
   I rest in your shelter,
   abide in your shadow,
   trust in you. Amen.

Proper 21

(Sunday between September 25 and October 1 inclusive)

COMPLEMENTARY

Amos 6:1a, 4–7	1 Timothy 6:6–19
Psalm 146	Luke 16:19–31

OPENING WORDS / CALL TO WORSHIP

Happy are those whose help is in the God of Jacob,   *Ps. 146:5, 10*
whose hope is in the Lord their God.
The Lord God reigns forever,
for all generations.
Praise the Lord!

CALL TO CONFESSION

If we call out in need,   *Ps. 146:7*
the Lord will answer.
Let us confess our sins against God and our neighbor,
trusting in the Lord who sets prisoners free.

PRAYER OF CONFESSION

We have sinned, O God,   *1 Tim. 6:9–10;*
hoarding what we have,   *Luke 16:19–20*
grasping for more,
and ignoring those who hunger and thirst.
We stay with our own kind;
we are complacent in the face of systems that oppress.
Forgive us;
purify us;
remake us,
that we might love as you love. Amen.

DECLARATION OF FORGIVENESS

The Lord welcomes all   *1 Tim. 6:12*
who return from the exile of greed and self-interest.

Be at peace,
for in Christ we find our way home again
where all are forgiven, loved, and restored.

PRAYER OF THE DAY

Loving God, giver of all good gifts,   *1 Tim. 6:6–19*
you have created us for life together,
and in Christ you have revealed to us
that the true riches of faith are good works,
generosity, and a desire to serve.
Strengthen us this day to pursue all righteousness,
    godliness, and love
with perseverance and gentleness,
that we may take hold of the life that is really life,
and dwell with you eternally. **Amen.**

PRAYER FOR ILLUMINATION

Nurturing God,   *1 Tim. 6:13; Luke 16:21*
you give life to all things
and long to satisfy the needs of your children
in their desire for healing and wholeness.
Send your Spirit upon us this day,
that as we hear your word we may meet Jesus,
the one in whom all our hungers are fed. **Amen.**

PRAYERS OF INTERCESSION

[optional response to each intercession:]
Answer us, O Lord, when we call on you;   *Ps. 91:15–16*
show us your salvation.

Hear our prayer, O Lord,   *Ps. 91*
our refuge and fortress,
our God, in whom we trust:

For those who are under siege   *Jer. 32*
from war or illness or any adversity—
give them faith and hope
for the future you are preparing.

For those who live in fear   *Ps. 91*
of terror in the night

or destruction in the day—
be with them in trouble
and satisfy them with long life.

For those who live in comfort and ease,   *Amos 6*
satisfied with gluttony, drunk with power,
wasting their days with idle pastimes—
show them the evil of their ways
and the end that is coming if they do not repent.

For those who are hungry or oppressed,   *Ps. 146*
those in prison, or burdened by heavy labor,
for the orphan, the widow, and the immigrant—
give them food and freedom, justice and joy,
watch over them and show them your welcome.

Merciful God, we offer you these prayers   *Luke 16*
in the confidence that you alone
have the grace to receive us
and the power to deliver us;
through Jesus Christ,
who has risen from the dead. **Amen.**

INVITATION TO THE OFFERING

We bring nothing into this world,   *1 Tim. 6*
and when we depart from this life
we will take nothing out of it.
All that we have is a gift from God;
therefore let us offer our lives to the Lord.

PRAYER OF THANKSGIVING/DEDICATION

We give you thanks and praise, generous God,   *1 Tim. 6*
for every good gift that comes from your hand:
for food and clothing,
for life and health,
for family and friends,
above all for the treasure of your grace.
Make us rich in good works,
generous and ready to share,
taking hold of the life

that really is life;
through Jesus Christ our Lord. **Amen.**

CHARGE

Pursue righteousness, godliness,   *1 Tim. 6*
faith, love,
endurance, gentleness.
Take hold of the eternal life
to which you were called.

BLESSING

May the sovereign Lord bless you,   *1 Tim. 6:15*
may the Christ of mercy keep you,
and the Holy Spirit sustain you,
in this life and the life to come.

Question for Reflection

What is wealth to God?

Household Prayer: Morning

God of radiance and glory
you give life to all things
and call us to life everlasting.
Show us the treasure of your grace
so that we may take hold
of the life that really is life;
through Christ Jesus, Lord of lords. Amen.

Household Prayer: Evening

Most High God,
in the shadow of your wings
there is nothing to fear.
Cover us with your grace this night.
Be with us in trouble,
satisfy us with long life,
and show us your saving love;
through Jesus Christ our Lord. Amen.

Proper 22

(Sunday between October 2 and October 8 inclusive)

SEMICONTINUOUS

Lamentations 1:1–6	2 Timothy 1:1–14
Lamentations 3:19–26 *or* Psalm 137	Luke 17:5–10

OPENING WORDS / CALL TO WORSHIP
Destruction and violence are everywhere; *Hab. 1:3, 4*
strife and contention are all around.
The needs of the world are so great;
O Lord, increase our faith. *Luke 17:5*
The law is slack,
and justice does not prevail.
The needs of the world are so great;
O Lord, increase our faith.
How many threats surround us:
warfare, homelessness, loneliness, loss.
The needs of the world are so great,
but you, O God, are greater still—
the One in whom all things are possible. *Luke 1:37*
O Lord, increase our faith in you! *Luke 17:5*

CALL TO CONFESSION
God answers those who seek mercy; *Lam. 3:25–26*
salvation comes to those who wait for the Lord.
Therefore, let us confess
all we have done,
and what we have not done,
trusting in God's grace.

PRAYER OF CONFESSION
Merciful God, you have called us to live
in sincere faith *2 Tim. 1:5–8;*
and to suffer for the gospel. *Luke 17:5*

193

We confess that we do not come before you
with a clear conscience.
Our faith is clouded by sin and uncertainty.
We shrink from your call to live sacrificially
    on behalf of others.
Too quickly, we seek our own ease and comfort first.
We confess that in our own lives, and in the church,
we rely on our power rather than yours.
Forgive us, we pray,
for we are fractured and fearful disciples.
Take away from us a spirit of cowardice,
and restore to us the spirit of power rightly used,
of love unconditionally offered,
and of self-discipline gracefully lived.
In new mercy, forgive us and increase our faith,
that we may be faithful servants at your table.
In Christ's name we pray. Amen.

DECLARATION OF FORGIVENESS
The power of God,   *2 Tim. 1*
    has saved us:
    grace is given to us
    in Christ Jesus,
    who abolished death
    and brought life
    and immortality to light.

PRAYER OF THE DAY
Faithful Lord,
    present in sorrow,
    present in hope,
    allow our lament
    with space to seek you,
that we may not forget
    that your steadfast love never ceases
    and your Spirit forever flows. **Amen.**

PRAYER FOR ILLUMINATION
Holy God, speak your word;
let those who hear

guard the good treasure
entrusted to them
with the help of the Holy Spirit,
living in us all. **Amen.**

[or]

Faithful God,   *Lam. 3:25;*
we wait in hope for you to speak.   *Luke 17:5, 9*
Come to us in Scripture read and proclaimed.
By the power of your Holy Spirit,
increase our faith
that we may do all we are commanded to do
according to your glory. **Amen.**

PRAYER OF LAMENT

*[may be spoken by one person, alternated between one person
and the assembly, or prayed antiphonally by the assembly]*
Present Lord,   *Lam. 1*
    how lonely sits the city,
    alleyways erode without games or even mischief.
    What was once great among the nations,
    holding backyard baseball and neighborhood parties,
    has become a vassal,
    a faded photograph.
    She weeps bitterly in the night,
    left alone to the distant sound of one more screen door slam.
    She has no one to comfort her,
    knowing another has left for good.
    They have become her enemies,
    through death or desertion.
    Judah has gone into exile,
    along with the words "hope" and "future."
    She finds no resting place,
    for danger lies with the abandoned.
    Her pursuers have all overtaken her,
    symbolized by the tall weeds in her lawn.
    The roads to Zion mourn,
    sidewalks split and bulge.
    The priests groan,
    churches are boarded up.

Young girls grieve,
throwing rocks at abandoned window panes.
Her foes have become the masters,
depression and victimhood moved in;
because the Lord made her suffer
a badge of punishment she wears in search of balance.
Her children have all gone away,
to a place where someday they will pay the same ransom.
From daughter Zion has departed all her majesty;
no one turns their heads, much less thinks to listen.
Like stags that find no pasture,
authorities find no subjects.
They fled without strength,
waiting to die.
Be present Lord. **Amen.**

INVITATION TO THE OFFERING

The Lord is our portion. *Lam. 3*
Therefore have hope
as you bring your gifts to God.

PRAYER OF THANKSGIVING/DEDICATION

Lord, your steadfast love never ceases;
your mercies never come to an end.
Use these gifts, we pray,
that through them your compassion may be known. **Amen.**

CHARGE

Go forth, *2 Tim. 1*
relying on the power of God,
who saved us
and called us
to a holy calling,
not according to our works,
but to God's purpose and grace.
[or]
Live with hope *Lam. 3:21–22, 26*
in the steadfast love of God.
Proclaim to all in despair
that God's mercies never come to an end.

In every circumstance,
wait on the Lord
who brings salvation.

BLESSING

May God restore the road before you
that leads to grace, mercy, and peace;
may Christ fill you with the treasure
of faith and love;
and may the Holy Spirit help you
to live in hope, now and forever.

Questions for Reflection

In Luke 17:5–10, the disciples ask Jesus to increase their faith. By asking
this, they acknowledge that faith does not grow by our own works and
hard efforts but is a gift from God's grace. How has the gift of faith in your
own life changed over time? Was there a particular time when your faith
weakened? Can you recall a time when the strength of your faith helped
you endure? God often uses special people in our lives to help us grow in
faith and understanding. Who has helped you grow in faith?

Household Prayer: Morning

Silent sunrise sanctuary—
a dome of shelter
for the birth of day.
Birds and bugs begin—
an opposite of lullaby
proclaiming life anew.
We wake in wonder—
discerning between dream and daylight
a mystery ends, another begins.
Sunshine scatters shadows—
a heathery view
melting gray morning mist.
Never ceasing, never ending—
God's mercies
new each morning. Amen.

Household Prayer: Evening

dusk
to dark
to full moon brightness
blue night sky
speckling of stars and planets
white lights
forever patterned
read and known
but you knew them first
and through them
allowed yourself to become known
Thank You
Praise You
and Goodnight.
Amen.

Proper 22

(Sunday between October 2 and October 8 inclusive)

COMPLEMENTARY

Habakkuk 1:1–4; 2:1–4   2 Timothy 1:1–14
Psalm 37:1–9   Luke 17:5–10

OPENING WORDS / CALL TO WORSHIP

In the midst of war and division,   *Lam. 1:2–4; 3:22–23*
we wait for God:
**The steadfast love of the Lord never ceases,
God's mercies never come to an end.**
In the midst of devastation and loss,
we wait for God:
**The steadfast love of the Lord never ceases,
God's mercies never come to an end.**
In the midst of change and uncertainty,
we wait for God:
**The steadfast love of the Lord never ceases,
God's mercies never come to an end;
they are new every morning.
Great is your faithfulness, O God!**

CALL TO CONFESSION

We turn to God in praise and prayer   *Col. 1:20*
not from a position of power and strength,
but from the broken edges of our lives,
from the broken edges of the world and the church.
We offer our prayers of confession,
trusting in the One who is reconciling all things.*

---

*Inspired by Beth Laneel Tanner's "Exegetical Perspective" on Lamentations 3:19–26, Proper 22, in ibid., 133.

PRAYER OF CONFESSION

Merciful God, *Lam. 1:2–4*
we confess that the world suffers because of our sin.
We use power against others for our own benefit.
We misuse the natural resources of the earth
in carelessness and greed.
By our habits and apathies,
others are subjected to desolation, even despair.
Forgive us for making enemies and exiles
of those you call us to love and serve.
Forgive us for laying waste to the landscape of creation.
Forgive us for being complicit in causing others to grieve
and to wander without rest.
We wait on you, O God.
We hope in you.
You alone can restore all things, even us.
We pray in Christ's name. Amen.

DECLARATION OF FORGIVENESS

God, in Christ Jesus, *2 Tim. 1*
grants us grace, mercy, and peace.
Let us hold to the sound teaching of the faith:
that God has the power to save us
and has given us grace through all the ages.
We receive the treasure of faith entrusted to us,
with the help of the Holy Spirit living in us.
Thanks be to God!

PRAYER OF THE DAY

God of our salvation, *2 Tim. 1*
we thank you for the gift of faith.
We thank you for all those who have taught us the good news.
Kindle in us always this gift, this good treasure,
that we may live the life to which you have called us,
according to your purpose and grace.
We pray in the name of the one
who abolished death
and brought life to light
through the gospel,
our Savior Christ Jesus. **Amen.**

PRAYER FOR ILLUMINATION

Holy God, through Christ Jesus   *2 Tim. 1:5, 10, 14*
you bring the light of the gospel
into our lives as grace revealed.
Help us to guard this treasure
and to share it with others, too,
so that the faith that has lived in our ancestors
and now lives in us
may come to life in every new generation.
We pray with the help of the Holy Spirit
who lives in us. **Amen.**

PRAYERS OF INTERCESSION

Let us pray for the needs of the world, saying,
Great is your faithfulness; O God, we hope in you.
[The leader may gesture to the assembly to indicate the response.]

God of grace and God of glory,
you care for the whole earth;
even now you are reconciling all things to yourself.   *Col. 1:20*
We thank you for the ancient grace
given in Christ Jesus before the ages began.   *2 Tim. 1:9c*
As age has succeeded age to this present day
your grace is with us still.
We rely on your power for all things.   *2 Tim. 1:8*
Great is your faithfulness; **O God, we hope in you.**   *Lam. 3:23–24*

We bring before you now the cares of the world.
We pray for people enduring the devastation of war
and oppression from enemies.
We pray for cities and for public life
that has suffered destruction and ruin.   *Lam. 1:1–6*
Bring restoration, we pray,
and an end to conflicts that divide and destroy.
Great is your faithfulness; **O God, we hope in you.**

We pray for nations and peoples undergoing turmoil and struggle.
Return us to your ways of justice and truth.
Give us compassionate hearts and resolute spirits
as we work to repair community and offer solace.

where now there is no resting place.
Great is your faithfulness; **O God, we hope in you.**   *Lam. 1:3b*

God of tender mercy,
you hear the cries of the one who is suffering,
of the one trying to recover,
of the one who has been hurt by another,
of one at risk in a complex and impersonal system.
Enfold each one in your steadfast love.
Take special care of those who do not, or cannot, cry out,
but wait quietly in hope.   *Lam. 3:26*
Give voice to those who should not wait quietly;
empower them with strength and support all around:
the powerless one who suffers abuse;
the person who is lonely, with no one to help;
the one who wanders homeless among us, unnoticed;
the one carrying an old burden, a silent grief,
     or an unvoiced fear.
With the gift of life given in the soaring light
     of your gospel   *2 Tim. 1:10*
abolish the daily death they bear,
Great is your faithfulness; **O God, we hope in you.**

We pray for your church, so in need of healing
     and reconciliation.
Rekindle in us the sincere faith of Christ   *2 Tim. 1:5*
and make us willing and faithful servants.   *Luke 17:5–10*
In unmerited grace, in startling new mercy,
you chose to call us not servants, but friends.   *John 15:15*
You have opened to us a place at your table of grace.
We would be good stewards of your grace
and glad of the company you call us to keep around
     your table,
which is larger than we have yet imagined.
In gratitude for the bread and cup you share,
we will honor you by sharing our bread with others,
by offering without reserve the cup you bless.
Great is your faithfulness; **O God, we hope in you.**
In the name of our Savior, Jesus Christ, we pray. **Amen.**

INVITATION TO THE OFFERING

Before us is a world in great need, waiting in hope.
We are a people holding treasure meant to be given away:
the good news of Christ;
resources of time, talents, and money.
If we are to participate in God's steadfast love and mercy,
we must give sacrificially to the needs of God's people.

PRAYER OF THANKSGIVING/DEDICATION

Gracious God, you are good news for a weary world.   *2 Tim. 1:9*
You are hope for people in despair,
    and you are home to exiles.
Accept, we pray, the offerings we bring this day.
Use them according to your own purpose and grace.
In Christ's name we ask it. **Amen.**

CHARGE

Fulfill your holy calling   *2 Tim. 1:9;*
by serving God and serving neighbor   *Luke 17:7–10*
without thought of reward.
And hope always in God,
through whom all things are possible.

BLESSING

May the steadfast love of God be upon you.
May the grace of Christ Jesus our Lord be within you.
May the abiding presence of the Holy Spirit uphold you,
now and forever.

Question for Reflection

What is faith?

Household Prayer: Morning

New every morning are your mercies, dear God.
As I begin this new day,
make me as merciful to others as you have been to me.
Strengthen me in faith
so that I may trust in you with my whole heart.

If any trouble overtakes me today,
help me to wait and to hope in you.
May the Holy Spirit help me
as I both guard and give away to others
the treasure of Jesus Christ, my Savior. Amen.

Household Prayer: Evening

God of my homecoming,
the night falls with your steadfast love
watching over the world.
I put my trust in you as I prepare to lie down in sleep.
Thank you for the gift of the day as it has been:
for glimpses of beauty;
for expressions of care;
for opportunities to serve.
Thank you for the gift of faith kindled and rekindled in me through
    the years.
Thank you for those who have taught me the faith
    in sincerity and love.
With the return of morning's light,
may I rise from this resting place
to live tomorrow in accord with your purpose and grace.
In Jesus' name, I pray. Amen.

Proper 23

(Sunday between October 9 and October 15 inclusive)

SEMICONTINUOUS

Jeremiah 29:1, 4–7	2 Timothy 2:8–15
Psalm 66:1–12	Luke 17:11–19

OPENING WORDS / CALL TO WORSHIP

[Shouting]

Come and see what God has done.   *Ps. 66*
God is awesome in God's deeds.
God turned the sea into dry land.
God's people passed through the river on foot.
Make a joyful noise to God all the earth.
Sing the glory of God's name.

[Singing]

Glory be to the Father, and to the Son, and to the Holy Ghost.
As it was in the beginning, is now, and ever shall be,
     world without end.
Amen. Amen.

[or]

Make a joyful noise to God, all the earth;   *Ps. 66*
sing the glory of God's name.
How awesome are your deeds, O God!
We sing praises to your name.
Come and see what God has done:
turning the sea into dry land;
bringing us across the river Jordan.
How awesome are your deeds, O God!
We sing praises to your name.
Even when God has tested us;
even when we have gone through fire and water:
God has brought us out to a spacious place.
Our God is an awesome God!

CALL TO CONFESSION

Even when we are faithless, Christ remains faithful.
Trusting in grace, let us confess our sins.

PRAYER OF CONFESSION

Jesus, Master, *Luke 17*
have mercy on us.
We keep our distance from you,
    for we are broken and sick with sin.
Yet you see us, and cleanse us, and make us whole.
Forgive us when we forget to return to you—
    have mercy when we fail to praise your name,
    and help us to exude the faith that makes us well. Amen.

DECLARATION OF FORGIVENESS

Hear the good news:
Your call has been answered.
Christ has healed you,
and forgives your sin.
With glad hearts, return praise to God. *Luke 17*

[Singing]
Praise God, from whom all blessings flow;
Praise God, all creatures here below;
Praise God above, ye heavenly hosts;
Praise Father, Son, and Holy Ghost. Amen.

PRAYER OF THE DAY

Past, Present, and Future God, *Jer. 29*
Creator, Sustainer, Redeemer,
help us to remember home and to hope in the promised land,
that we might know you,
Alpha and Omega,
Three in One.
Amen.

PRAYER FOR ILLUMINATION

These are *Jer. 29*
    your words
      O, God.

Humble us
  to speak
  their weight.
Strengthen us
  to hear
  their truth.
Unbind us
  to live
  their call.

Through the power of your Holy Spirit,
for the sake of Jesus Christ, we pray. **Amen.**

[or]

Your Word, O God, is not chained;   *2 Tim. 2*
send your Spirit, that by this Word we may be set free.

PRAYER OF LAMENT

Joblessness, homelessness, hopelessness, and sorrow,   *Jer. 29*
unloved, unsafe, oppressed, and injured,
un-led, unbelieving, alone, and lonely—

You sent us into exile—
a place defined by "other," against, "stolen home."
You ask us to settle in—
to succumb to treason and defeat.
You want our generations to be born here—
we fear their trauma more than our own.
You ask us to seek welfare from this city—
have we not borne injustice enough?
You ask us to pray peace for this place—
we become indignant and angry.
Yet pray we must—
peace, peace, peace!

INVITATION TO THE OFFERING

Have you looked in awe   *Ps. 66*
  at the roundness of raindrops
  or the conical shape of spruce
  or the multitude of human forms
  or the contours of a cloud?

What was once formless and void
    has been transformed into a spacious place.
Let us give in all shapes and forms
    for the sake of God's creation
    and all who dwell in it.

PRAYER OF THANKSGIVING/DEDICATION
Small and humble in comparison
    we give to you
    that you might mold
    our world anew. **Amen.**

CHARGE AND BLESSING
Get up and go on your way, remembering to turn back
    in praise to God.   *Luke 17*
May you be blessed with faith and made well.
[or]
Step forth in joy.
Walk out in song.
All the earth, praise God,
for our God is an awesome God.

Questions for Reflection

In both the reading from Jeremiah and the reading from Luke, God is at
work not only among the chosen people of Israel, but also among those
considered enemies of Israel. God tells Israel to make its home among the
Babylonians while in exile, seeking the welfare of the city to which they
have been sent. Jesus heals a "double-outcast," a man who is a Samaritan
and a leper. Is there someone in your own life whom you feel is an "enemy"
to you—or someone you would rather not be associated with for some
reason? Who are enemies in a larger sphere (national, political, or social)?
How can you "seek their welfare"? How may you, in faith, reach out to such
a one?

Household Prayer: Morning

God of endings,
    of packing up
    decisions of keeping and leaving

of saying goodbye
the practice of closing and tidying
of moving
the finality of distance between
of newness,
the lonely silence of emptiness.
Grant me
the strength to start over.
Amen.

Household Prayer: Evening

Generous God,
    a day of worship
    a day of rest
    a day in community
    a day to be blessed

    a day for offering
    a day for welcoming
    a day of remembering
    a day of reckoning—

    this is the day
    the Lord has made.
    Let us rejoice
    and be glad in it.
Amen.

Proper 23

(Sunday between October 9 and October 15 inclusive)

COMPLEMENTARY

2 Kings 5:1–3, 7–15c   ✓2 Timothy 2:8–15
Psalm 111   ✓ Luke 17:11–19

OPENING WORDS / CALL TO WORSHIP

God has sent redemption to us   *Ps. 111*
and made with us a covenant.
Holy and awesome is God's name.
Praise the Lord!

CALL TO CONFESSION

Since Jesus Christ was a descendant of David,   *2 Tim. 2:8*
Christ shared our humanity.
He understands our struggles to be faithful.
Yet even when we are faithless,
Christ remains faithful.   —   *2 Tim. 2:13*
Jesus came not to condemn or exclude,
but to make us well,
to make us whole.   *Luke 17:19*
In his name we confess our sins and call out,
"Lord, have mercy on us!"   *Luke 17:13*

PRAYER OF CONFESSION

God of mercy and grace,   *Ps. 66:1*
we are meant to praise you and give thanks
     to you always.
We confess that we do not live out of
     constant gratitude.
We harbor resentment for what we lack.
We blame you; we blame others.
We doubt your compassion, even your power.

We find it hard to give ourselves away to you,
    or to others,
in generous expressions of gratitude and praise.
Forgive us, we pray,
for attitudes and behaviors that diminish in us
    joyful thanksgiving.
Heal and restore us so that we may return to you
    with a right spirit.
Help us to live holy and joyful lives,
befitting people you love and save.
We pray in Christ's name. Amen.

DECLARATION OF FORGIVENESS

In the waters of baptism,   *2 Tim. 2:11;*
we have died with Christ   *Rom. 8:38–39*
and we have been raised with him to new life.
Nothing in life or in death can separate us
from the love of God in Christ Jesus our Lord.
In Christ we are forgiven and set free
to live in praise and thanksgiving!
Thanks be to God!

PRAYER OF THE DAY

God of our salvation,   *Luke 17:16*
you are the source of wisdom and joy.
Your love and mercies are not limited
to one time or to one people.
You continue to heal and to save,
transcending the artificial boundaries and barriers we set.
For such expansive love,
it is our right, duty, and joy
to offer you all our thanks and praise,
now and forever. **Amen.**

PRAYER FOR ILLUMINATION

Sovereign God,   *2 Tim. 2:9, 15*
though we are bound by many tethers,
your Word is not chained.
Set us free by this Word
let loose in the world.

By the power of your Holy Spirit,
make us worthy of your approval:
workers of the gospel,
unashamed and unafraid to share
the truth made known to us.
In Christ Jesus, we pray. **Amen.**

PRAYERS OF INTERCESSION
[A brief silence may be kept after each intercession.]
We bless you, O God, for your power:
in mighty deeds and tender mercies.
We bless you, O God, for your watchful care:
    in places of exile and at home.
We bless you, O God, for your healing presence:
    in sickness and in brokenness.

We pray to you for the needs of the world:
for those enslaved by political, military, or social oppression . . .
for those suffering from violence and illnesses we can prevent . . .
for those at risk from famine, drought, and natural disasters. . . .

We pray to you for the renewing of creation:
for an end to harmful habits and willful ruin . . .
for heightened care for species at risk . . .
for more faithful stewardship among us toward earth's resources. . . .

We pray to you for the cares of our community:
for those who have lost jobs, homes, and hope . . .
for those who are hungry today and will be again tomorrow . . .
for those troubled in mind, body, or spirit, and for those recovering. . . .

We pray to you for the cares we hold this day:
for patience in difficulty . . .
for a renewal of commitment . . .
for grace to forgive ourselves or another. . . .

Heal us, we pray, in our dis-eases, estrangements,
and in the broken places of our lives.
May we return to you, to creation, and to community
in joy and thanksgiving according to your grace.

Give your church fresh courage and bold vision
in this changeful time,
as we pray for the welfare of all people.
In the name of the one who came to heal and to save,
Jesus the Christ. **Amen.**

INVITATION TO THE OFFERING
Practicing gratitude can change our lives as individuals;
it can change our life as a congregation.
In the spirit of gratitude to God,
our giving is not reduced to ethical duty
but is elevated to delight and joy.
As we offer to God these measured gifts,
let us also offer unmeasured praise.

PRAYER OF THANKSGIVING/DEDICATION
Like the shepherds in Bethlehem's field,   *Luke 2:8, 20*
like the leper healed who returned to Jesus,   *Luke 17:15–16*
like the Jews and Gentiles of the early church,   *Acts 2:46–47*
we praise and glorify your name, O God.
You have given us more than we could have imagined!
For tidings of joy, for wholeness received,
for the gift of belonging, we thank you.
Make of us, as well as these gifts,
offerings of good news to the poor,
hope to the hopeless,
and signs of your power to reconcile and redeem.
We ask all things in the name of Christ. **Amen.**

CHARGE
Practice the faith
by practicing gratitude to God
every day, in all circumstances;
for God is bringing us from death
to life.
[or]
Come and see what God has done,   *Ps. 66:5*
and give to God glorious praise.   *Ps. 66:2*
Seek the welfare of all, even your enemies.   *Jer. 29:7*
And remember Jesus Christ,   *2 Tim. 2:8*

giving thanks to him   *Luke 17:16*
for your salvation.

BLESSING

May God keep watch over us and all nations;   *Ps. 66:7*
may Christ restore us, body and soul;   *Luke17:11–19*
and may the Holy Spirit help us to remain faithful,   *2 Tim. 2:13*
giving thanks to God our whole life long.

Questions for Reflection

The Greek word for "Eucharist"—*eucharistia*—means *thanksgiving* and is
used in Luke 17:16 to describe the Samaritan's thankful response of faith
to Jesus, who had mercy on him. To live a "eucharistic life," then, is to
live a life of thanksgiving to God.* The Larger and Shorter Catechism of
the Westminster Standards (1647) both begin with a version of the same
question and answer:

Q. 1. What is the chief end of [humankind]?
A: [Our] chief end is to glorify God and to enjoy [God] forever.

Can you recount some of the ways in which you are glorifying and
enjoying God in your daily life? What new habits or practices might
cultivate in you a more eucharistic life?

Household Prayer: Morning

Glorious God, I praise you.
I praise you for who you are—
loving, merciful, powerful, and just.
I praise you for the ways you act in creation—
creating beauty, bringing freedom, making peace, offering healing.
Thank you for opportunities I will have today
to glorify you in my words and actions.

---

*These thoughts of the "eucharistic life" and the first question and answer of the Larger
Catechism and Shorter Catechism are from Margit Ernst-Habib's "Theological Perspective" on
Luke 17:11–19, Proper 23, in ibid., 166, 168.

Thank you for this very day in which I am able to enjoy you
by participating in your activity in the world.
I pray that the enmity between people and nations
may give way to true communion.
In the name of Christ, the great Reconciler, I pray. Amen.

Household Prayer: Evening

Loving God, I end this day as I began it—in praise of you.
Thank you for including me in your great circle of love and care.
Thank you for being with us always.
Thank you, too, for calling me to love others
and to treat everyone as my neighbor.
Help me to notice those whose cries for mercy
so often go unheard or unanswered,
for I am joined to them by being joined to you.
I pray in awe of the life you have given me
through faith in Jesus Christ. Amen.

Proper 24

SEMICONTINUOUS

Jeremiah 31:27–34   2 Timothy 3:14–4:5
Psalm 119:97–104   Luke 18:1–8

OPENING WORDS / CALL TO WORSHIP

No matter how far from God we seem to be,   *Jer. 31; 2 Tim. 3;*
we do not lose heart: *Luke 18*
For the days are surely coming, says the Lord.
No matter how many obstacles we face in life,
   in the church,
we do not lose heart:
For the days are surely coming, says the Lord.
No matter how hard it is to continually pray and
   work for justice,
we do not lose heart:
For the days are surely coming, says the Lord,
when I will forgive and restore my people;
when I will equip them for every good work;
and when I will grant justice,
for I hear their cries day and night.
[or]

How I love God's law!   *Ps. 119:98, 103;*
God's commandments and teachings   *Jer. 31:31–34;*
are always with me.   *2 Tim. 3:15–16*
How sweet are God's words to my taste,
sweeter than honey to my mouth!
God's new covenant is written on our hearts
so that we may all know God,
young and old, powerful and powerless alike.
How sweet are God's words to my taste,
sweeter than honey to my mouth!
In the Word we hear the good news of the gospel:

salvation is ours through faith in Christ Jesus.
How sweet are God's words to my taste,
sweeter than honey to my mouth!

CALL TO CONFESSION

The new covenant God has made with Israel,
    and with us,   *Jer. 31:31–34*
begins in forgiveness.
Though we continually break covenant with God,
God remains faithful.
We confess our sins to God,
    trusting that God will forgive us and remember
        our sins no more.

PRAYER OF CONFESSION

Gracious God,
we confess that we do not meditate on your commands
    and teachings
all day long.   *Ps. 119:97*
We do not keep your word before us always
    and in all things.   *Ps. 119:101*
Instead, we turn away from your demanding truth
and wander toward easier options.   *2 Tim. 3:3–4*
Forgive us, we pray,
for pursuing our own desires rather than yours.
Forgive us for growing weary in following you;
for failing to pray and work tirelessly for justice;   *Luke 18:7*
for losing hope in your power to transform the
    powers of this world.
Tune our ears to the sound of your justice.
Turn our hearts to your commandments and
    word of grace.
Do not remember our sin,   *Jer. 31:34*
but remember your mercy forever.
We pray in Christ's name. Amen.

DECLARATION OF FORGIVENESS

The Scriptures are given to correct our ways,   *2 Tim. 3:16–17; 4:1*
to train us in righteousness,
and to equip us for every good work.

In the presence of God and of Christ Jesus,
who is the only judge of the living and the dead,
we give thanks for the gift of forgiveness.
**By the grace of Christ, we will be persistent
in the life of faith to which we are called.**
[or]
Friends, God promises to forgive us,
to put our sins out of God's own mind and heart.
In this way, God gives us not just a second chance
but a new beginning.
Believe the good news of the gospel:
**our salvation is through faith in Christ Jesus.
Thanks be to God! Amen.**

PRAYER OF THE DAY

O God who writes on our hearts,   *Jer. 31:31–33; 2 Tim. 4:1*
you have never abandoned us.
In amazing and persistent grace,
you have kept covenant with us.
We thank you for loving us
even when we have not loved you.
We long to behold the day of your appearing,
even as we stand now in view of your kingdom,
promised and made present in Christ Jesus,
in whose name we wait and pray. **Amen.**
[or]
God of justice and mercy,   *Ps. 119:97; 2 Tim. 3:15–16;*
we thank you for the gift of the law   *Luke 18:7*
    and all the Scriptures.
We thank you for establishing justice
and for dealing with us not according to
    our faithfulness,
but according to your mercy.
Put your persistent Spirit within us
so that we may work tirelessly,
and cry out day and night,
until your will is done in all the earth.
We pray to you who helps us,
in the name of your Son, our Lord, Jesus Christ. **Amen.**

PRAYER FOR ILLUMINATION

Holy God,   *2 Tim. 3:16, 17; 4:2*
the words of Scripture are God-breathed words—
inspired by you
and given life
through the power of your Holy Spirit.
By your Spirit breathe your word into us,
so that we become proficient in the language of faith
and equipped to proclaim the message we receive,
for the sake of Jesus Christ,
the Living Word. **Amen.**

PRAYERS OF INTERCESSION

*[The prayers may be led by two people, each
speaking a section.]*
O God our Judge and our Redeemer,   *Luke 18:7, 8;*
we cry to you day and night. Help us, O God.   *2 Tim. 3:14; 4:3–4*

We thank you for all who have taught us the faith
     and who teach us still,
this faith that is a firm foundation for our lives
     and our life together.
We pray that you will continue to guide
     and bless the church
in yet another time of change and reformation.
Help us to trust in you so strongly
that we are willing to take risks for the gospel,
even if, in risking,
we grow uncomfortable or afraid of uncertainty
     and newness.
Keep us moving in concert with the Holy Spirit.
Give your church wisdom to discern sound teaching.
Never let us be satisfied with easy answers that
     do not follow your way.
O God, our Judge and our Redeemer,
we cry to you day and night. Help us, O God.

We bring to you the concerns and cares of the
world around us.

Especially we pray for those who long for justice
    and freedom,
safety and sustenance.
We pray for those who work to overturn laws
    that oppress,
and those who work to restrain military might
    that threatens human dignity.
We pray for people caught in unjust systems;
those being denied education and health care;
victims of human trafficking;
exiles who wander, lonely for home.
We pray for all who live daily with food insecurity
and job insecurity and peace insecurity.
We pray fervently for an end to war and violence
    among us.
We pray for an end to hunger and for an increase
    in generosity
as we share the world's resources.
We pray for all who are in harm's way today,
whether the threat is from natural disaster
    or a disaster of our own contriving.
O God, our Judge and our Redeemer,
we cry to you day and night. Help us, O God.

We bring to you the cares and joys of our lives.
We rejoice with those among us
who celebrate a time of newness and renewal:
for a new addition to the family;
for a new relationship bringing a sense of happiness
    and fun;
for meaningful work to do and good colleagues;
for new members and visitors among us
who bring energy and ideas and faith stories
that enrich our life together;
for healing and hope after a difficult time.
We pray, too, for those in the midst of struggle
    and pain:
those who are contending with illness;
ones in need of the comfort and peace that
only you, O Lord, can give.

We pray for those who are living with the
  anxiety of loss—
of income, of memory, or stability of home
  or friendship.
Heal us of our diseases;
strengthen us in our frailties;
and empower us for change.
O God, our Judge and our Redeemer,
we cry to you day and night. Help us, O God.

We do not cry out in desperation, but in hope;
for you are just in all your ways
and you hear us when we call upon you.
We pray that in us you may indeed find faith,
the faith of our Savior, Jesus Christ, living in us. **Amen.**

INVITATION TO THE OFFERING

The writer of Second Timothy calls us to "carry out
  your ministry fully."   *2 Tim. 3:17; 4:5*
Our ministry is most fully carried out when our
  hearts are full—
full of love, justice, and generosity
in sharing what we have with others.
Equipped for every good work,
we now present ourselves and our offerings before God.

PRAYER OF THANKSGIVING/DEDICATION

God of generous providing,   *Ps. 119;*
you have given us so many gifts that   *2 Tim. 3:15–17;*
  enrich our lives.   *Jer. 31:31–33*
The sacred writings that provide instruction,
  correction, and training;
the gift of the church;
covenantal love and faithfulness;
your own dear Son, Jesus Christ, our Savior;
the gift of the Spirit, our Advocate.
We belong to you, and all that we have belongs to you.
Use these offerings, we pray,
in service of the justice you are establishing
through your kingdom in Christ Jesus our Lord. **Amen.**

CHARGE

You belong to God,   *2 Tim. 3:17*
therefore I urge you:
stand firm in the faith,   *2 Tim. 3:14*
pray persistently,   *Luke 18:1*
and work tirelessly for justice,   *Luke 18:3*
for the days are surely coming   *Jer. 31:27, 31; 2 Tim. 4:3*
when God's kingdom will be all in all.   *2 Tim. 4:1*

[or}

God's steadfast covenant writes it:
The law of love in our hearts.
Christ's concern for the least demands it:
The cry of justice on our lips.
The Spirit's encouragement breathes it:
The living word within us.

BLESSING

May the love of God dwell in your heart;   *Jer. 31:33*
may the grace of Christ uphold you in faith;   *2 Tim. 3:14*
may the Holy Spirit equip you for ministry;   *2 Tim. 3:17; 4:5*
until Christ's kingdom,
already in view,   *2 Tim. 4:1*
comes in fullness among us.

[or}

May the presence of God,
the grace of Christ,
and the power of the Holy Spirit
sustain us in faith and service,
now and forever.

Questions for Reflection

Luke's parable of the widow (Luke 18:1–8) who continually came to the
judge seeking justice encourages us not to lose heart. We are to pray and to
be persistent in the life of faith on behalf of the justice God intends. God is
pictured in contrast to this unjust judge who doesn't care a bit about justice
but does care about his own peace of mind! God, of course, has no peace of
mind without justice. If we think of ourselves as the widow in this parable,
then few of us have her stamina in the hard, exhausting work of seeking
justice on behalf of the powerless. Perhaps this is the reason Jesus asks

the closing question of the parable: ". . . when the Son of Man comes, will he find faith on earth?" Will he find faith in us—persistent, tireless faith seeking justice? Margit Ernst-Habib* invites us to think that the widow represents not only our need to pray relentlessly but also to see the Holy Spirit in this insistent widow. The Spirit is at work, earnestly, unrelentingly encouraging us to pray. What causes you to lose hope in your own prayer life? What might the Spirit be urging you to pray and work for on behalf of someone else?

Household Prayer: Morning

God of justice,
you are at work this very day
on behalf of those who are poor, marginalized, and disregarded.
Fill me with the power of your Holy Spirit
so that I can begin this day
praying earnestly for someone who faces injustice.
Help me to see and to act upon an opportunity
to participate in your love and justice.
Give me the eyes and ears of faith
as I go about my daily routines,
walk the paths and hallways of my daily life,
and attend to news local and global.
Then, seeing and hearing through the light of Christ,
encourage me relentlessly to pray and work
without losing heart.
I ask it in the name of Jesus. Amen.

Household Prayer: Evening

God of mercy,
I come to you now with my energy running low
as the lights of the evening.
Like stars in the darkness,
I send out my prayers for justice to you.

---

*Margit Ernst-Habib, "Theological Perspective" on Luke 17:11–19, in ibid., 166, 168.

May this small effort of mine send a ray of hope,
however faint,
to someone facing the darkness of trial or terror tonight.
I know how strong evil and injustice still are in this world,
yet I know you are stronger than even the worst we can do.
So, I do not lose heart;
rather, my heart rests in gratitude to you:
for the gift of life,
for the comforts of faith and those who are family to me,
and for the hope you have given us all
in Christ's rising from the dead.
I pray this night for peace among all people,
in the name of him who came to bring peace
unlike any the world can give, Jesus Christ our Lord. Amen.

Proper 24

(Sunday between October 16 and October 22 inclusive)

COMPLEMENTARY

Genesis 32:22-31   2 Timothy 3:14–4:5
Psalm 121   Luke 18:1–8

OPENING WORDS / CALL TO WORSHIP

Our help is in the name of the Lord,   *Ps. 121:2*
who made heaven and earth.
Sisters and brothers,
let us worship God.

CALL TO CONFESSION

[spoken from the font]
In spite of our best efforts to live faithfully,
we fall short of what God intends for us.
Because God has already promised to be merciful,
we dare to tell the truth about our lives.
In humility and trust, let us confess our sin.

PRAYER OF CONFESSION

God of grace,
For our failure to love others as you have loved us,
forgive us.

For wasting your gifts and hoarding our goods,
forgive us.

For losing heart and abandoning hope,
forgive us.

For all the ways we turn from you,
forgive us . . . .
[silent prayer]

We offer our prayers in the name of the One who saves us,
Jesus Christ. **Amen.**

DECLARATION OF FORGIVENESS
[Water is poured into the font.]
Grace flows like a river;
mercy like a never-ending stream.
Believe the good news:
in Jesus Christ we are forgiven.

PRAYER OF THE DAY
Eternal God,   *Gen. 32:24; Luke 18:1–8*
you remain constant through all of our striving,
and patient with our ceaseless prayers.
We seek your wisdom,
yearn for your justice,
and crave your blessing,
for our own sakes and for the sake of the world.
By the power of the Holy Spirit
and in the name of Christ, who prays with us. **Amen.**

PRAYER FOR ILLUMINATION
Speak to us,
by the power of your Holy Spirit,
and equip us to be messengers
of your life-altering,
world-changing,
blessing-filled Word.
Through Jesus Christ we pray. **Amen.**

PRAYERS OF INTERCESSION
[Silence may be kept after each intercession.]
God of justice,
in Jesus Christ you teach us to pray always and
    not to lose heart.   *Luke 18:1*
And so we come.

For your children who suffer under oppressive rulers
    and greedy tycoons . . .

For your church that is torn asunder by mistrust and pride . . .

For those who have no water and those whose water is too
dirty to drink . . .

For those who go to bed hungry and wake each day in misery . . .

For those who struggle to believe and those who seek a blessing . . .

For those who are bound by anxiety or depression, loneliness or fear . . .

For the sick and all who care for them and those who will
    die this night . . .

For all whose burdens we carry in our hearts, who we
    now name to you. . . .

All these prayers we offer with thanksgiving,
through the power of your own Spirit,
for we know that you hear us when we pray
and desire to makes us whole.
In the name of Jesus Christ, our Redeemer and Lord. **Amen.**

INVITATION TO THE OFFERING

Our God, who provides for our every need,
invites us to give of ourselves
as we work and wait for the coming reign of Christ.
Trusting in the Spirit to sustain us in all things,
let us share generously with those in need.

PRAYER OF THANKSGIVING/DEDICATION

Eternal God,
may these gifts be signs of your grace,   *Luke 18:8*
and may our lives show forth the coming kingdom,
that when Christ comes again he will find faith on earth. **Amen.**

CHARGE

Hear Paul's encouragement to the church in Philippi   *Phil. 4:6*
as a charge also to us:
Do not worry about anything,

but in everything by prayer and supplication
with thanksgiving let your requests be made known to God.

BLESSING

Be of good courage, *Ps. 121:8*
for the Lord will keep our going out
and our coming in
from this time on and forevermore.

Questions for Reflection

"I will not let you go," said Jacob to the night stranger, "unless you bless me." What does it mean to struggle for a blessing—from others or from God? How does that struggle manifest itself in your life?

Household Prayer: Morning

Thank you, gracious God,
for giving me a limp.
You have let me struggle with you;
you have blessed me;
you have marked me as your own.
Send me out today,
with all my frailties and weaknesses,
to be a witness to your love,
grateful for another day
to sing your praise. Amen.

Household Prayer: Evening

I lift up my eyes to the hills—from where will my help come? *Ps. 121*
My help comes from the LORD, who made heaven and earth.
God will not let your foot be moved; the One who keeps
    you will not slumber.
God who keeps Israel will neither slumber nor sleep.
The LORD is your keeper; the LORD is your shade at your right hand.
The sun shall not strike you by day, nor the moon by night.
The LORD will keep you from all evil; he will keep your life.
The LORD will keep your going out and your coming in
from this time on and forevermore. Amen.

Proper 25

(Sunday between October 23 and October 29 inclusive)

SEMICONTINUOUS

Joel 2:23–32	2 Timothy 4:6–8, 16–18
Psalm 65	Luke 18:9–14

OPENING WORDS / CALL TO WORSHIP

By awesome deeds you answer us with deliverance,   *Ps. 65:5–8*
O God of our salvation;
you are the hope of all the ends of the earth and
    of the farthest seas.
By your strength you established the mountains;
you are girded with might.
You silence the roaring of the seas,
    the roaring of their waves,
    the tumult of the peoples.

Those who live at earth's farthest bounds are awed
    by your signs;
you make the gateways of the morning and the
    evening shout for joy.

CALL TO CONFESSION

Even before we admit our sin,   *Joel 2:32*
God promises to hear us with mercy.
Everyone who calls on the name of the Lord shall be saved.

PRAYER OF CONFESSION

No words can express the depth of our need   *Ps. 65:3;*
or reveal the extent of our sin.   *2 Tim. 4:18*
But you know us completely, O God.

When deeds of iniquity overwhelm us,
you forgive our transgressions.
You rescue us from evil
and clothe us with love.
Humbly, we thank you;
for no words can express our gratitude
for the gift of your salvation. Amen.

DECLARATION OF FORGIVENESS

[Water is poured into the font, visibly and audibly.]
Sisters and brothers,   *2 Tim. 4:17*
the news is so good we can scarcely believe it:
God does not hold our sin against us
but pours out abundant grace.
Give thanks to God
and by the Spirit's power
share the gospel far and near:
In Jesus Christ we are forgiven!

PRAYER OF THE DAY

Good and gracious God,   *Joel 2:28; Ps. 65:5;*
you promise to pour out your Spirit upon us;   *Luke 18:14*
you are the hope of the world.
Give us strength, that we might serve you;
make us humble, that we might live for your glory alone.
In the name of Jesus we pray. **Amen.**

PRAYER FOR ILLUMINATION

Lord, to whom shall we go?   *John 6:68;*
You have the words of eternal life.   *2 Tim. 4:18*
By your Spirit make yourself known to us
through the reading and preaching of your Word,
that we might be faithful witnesses in this life
and joyful companions in the next,
even with Jesus, in whose name we pray. **Amen.**

PRAYERS OF INTERCESSION

[A time of silence may follow each intercession.]
Holy God,   *Joel 2; Ps. 65:2;*
you promise to hear us when we pray,   *2 Tim. 4*

and shower us with unexpected blessings.
You relieve our sufferings
and fill us with good things.
When we face challenges that threaten to overcome us,
you give us strength.
With grateful hearts, we entrust our cares and concerns to you,
praying, "Gracious God, hear our prayer."

For an end to violence,
between countries, within nations, on our streets, and in our homes,
and especially in *N.*
Gracious God, **hear our prayer.**

For those who offer aid to refugees and victims of natural disasters,
and all who suffer from forces beyond their control . . .
Gracious God, **hear our prayer.**

For those who seek shelter on the streets of our nation,
even in our own communities . . .
Gracious God, **hear our prayer.**

For all those who have lost their way . . .
Gracious God, **hear our prayer.**

For our Muslim neighbors, and peace between our peoples . . .
Gracious God, **hear our prayer.**

For our secret burdens . . .
Gracious God, **hear our prayer.**

Gather up our prayers, O God, and those we did not know to pray,
and make us ever more faithful as we lean into your coming reign
of justice, peace, and love;
through Jesus Christ, our light and our hope. **Amen.**

INVITATION TO THE OFFERING
God has delivered us by awesome deeds!   *Ps. 65:5*
With gratitude and joy,
let us bring our gifts of thanksgiving and love.

PRAYER OF THANKSGIVING/DEDICATION

God of creation,
you water the earth and send forth food;
you shower us with grace and feed us with your love.
Accept these gifts,
humble though they may be,
and use them to spread your goodness throughout the earth;
in Jesus' name we pray. **Amen.**

CHARGE

Have courage;   *2 Tim. 4:7, 17*
keep the faith;
rely on the strength that comes from God.

BLESSING

May the Creator nurture you,
the Teacher walk with you,
and the Spirit strengthen you,
this day and forevermore.

Questions for Reflection

The author of Second Timothy declares, "I have fought the good fight, I
have finished the race, I have kept the faith" (4:7). What does that look like
in your life? How does your church keep the faith, even in the face of all
the world's challenges?

Household Prayer: Morning

God of light,
thank you for another day.
With each hour,
may I be watchful for signs of your grace,
ready to show your love,
and eager to tell the good news of Jesus Christ.
Make me more faithful than I was yesterday,
and lead me in the paths of righteousness. Amen.

Household Prayer: Evening

Thank you for the challenges and blessings of this day, O God.
If I kept faith with you, thank you for your Spirit's help.
If I looked away from you, turn me back around.
As night falls, I relinquish my pride and my fear
and entrust all whom I love to your care,
with prayers for a peaceful rest;
in Jesus' name. Amen.

Proper 25

(Sunday between October 23 and October 29 inclusive)

COMPLEMENTARY

Sirach 35:12–17 *or*   2 Timothy 4:6–8, 16–18
   Jeremiah 14:7–10, 19–22   Luke 18:9–14
Psalm 84:1–7

OPENING WORDS / CALL TO WORSHIP

How lovely is your dwelling place, O Lord of hosts!   *Ps. 84:1–2, 4–5*
My soul longs for the courts of the Lord.
My flesh sings for joy to the living God.
Happy are those who live in the house of the Lord,
ever singing your praise, O God.
Happy are those whose strength is in you,
in whose heart are the highways to Zion.

CALL TO CONFESSION

Longing for rescue from the weight of our failures,
let us confess our sin to God who hears our pleas
and waits in mercy to forgive.

PRAYER OF CONFESSION

Merciful God, hope of your people in every age,
we confess that we have sinned against you.
We have wandered from your pathways,
turned toward idols,
lived without compassion,
and disregarded the well-being of your creation.
Do not turn away from us, O Lord,
but renew your covenant,
for only in you will our lives be healed.
Guide us and lead us in your ways,
for happy are those who live in your house. Amen.

DECLARATION OF FORGIVENESS

In the name of the One who yearns
to crown all people with righteousness
and whose mercy exalts the humble,
your sins are forgiven.
May you be strengthened to live
in the freedom of God's holy and eternal generosity. **Amen.**

PRAYER OF THE DAY

Righteous and gracious Lord,
you reveal to us the way of goodness and life.
Teach us humility
that we may trust in your power, and not our own,
and make us ever grateful;
in Jesus' name we pray. **Amen.**

PRAYER FOR ILLUMINATION

Pour out upon us your Spirit, O God,
that we might hear your word
so that your wisdom will draw us closer to you.
Through Christ, the Living Word, we pray. **Amen.**

PRAYERS OF INTERCESSION

Let us pray for the church, the world, and all in need, saying:
God of mercy, hear our prayer.

We pray for the church in every place,
that wherever people gather in your name,
you enable us to listen to each other with open hearts.
Give your people unity, O God;
replace pride with reconciliation.
God of mercy, **hear our prayer.**

We pray for musicians and artists,
Sunday school teachers and learners,
ushers, greeters, church council members,
secretaries, cooks and cleaners, student leaders,
deacons and presbyters, pastors and bishops,
and for all who serve your people.
God of mercy, **hear our prayer.**

We pray for Muslims and Jews, Hindus and Buddhists,
and people of indigenous religions everywhere,
that their paths may lead—with ours—
to greater understanding of the goodness of faith
in its many languages and forms.
God of mercy, **hear our prayer.**

We thank you for this amazing Earth,
for rich soils, abundant sunshine,
and all the foods that you have made for our health and enjoyment.
We thank you for clean waters,
especially for the waters of our region
*[Here name the lakes, seas, or rivers and creeks that are most vital to the
water table in your region.]*
Make us grateful for your gifts so that we protect what we have.
God of mercy, **hear our prayer.**

Reassure us, O God, that you desire good for your world
and all the people in it,
and that your provisions are sufficient.
Infuse us with a commitment to share with others,
especially with those who do not have such riches
and who today are hungry.
God of mercy, **hear our prayer.**

We pray for the leaders of our nation:
for our president and Congress;
for the leaders who struggle with drought and famine,
destructive storms and lack of food or shelter;
for leaders of peace movements
and for those who do not know how to create just societies;
for all who are suffering from the horrors of war,
especially for children who do not know the reason for their pain
and have no power to change their situations;
for soldiers, for dictators, for diplomats
and for those who pray each day for the welfare of others.
God of mercy, **hear our prayer.**

We pray for those suffering
from all forms of injustice, brokenness, or illness,

especially all who have asked for the prayers of this congregation
and for those whose well-being we hold in our hearts.
God of mercy, **hear our prayer.**

We pray for those concerns we name now aloud or silently . . .
*[Let there be enough time for silence to give everyone who might
speak a chance to do so.]*
God of mercy, **hear our prayer.**

God of eternity,
we know that all days are redeemed and held in your grace.
We remember with honor and gratitude
all those whose lives have enriched ours,
and especially those whose faith has given shape to our own.
Keep alive within us the hope of the resurrection.
God of mercy, **hear our prayer.**

Into your hands, O Lord, we commend all for whom we pray,
trusting in your mercy through your Son,
Jesus Christ, our Lord. **Amen.**

INVITATION TO THE OFFERING
With humility for all that God has given us,
let us gratefully give for the work of the church
and the healing of this world.

PRAYER OF THANKSGIVING/DEDICATION
Holy and merciful God,
you know the joy that is in us
when we offer ourselves, our time, and our possessions
for the work you set before us.
Use these gifts to heal and teach, comfort and challenge,
that all the world might give you praise. **Amen.**
[or]
Let us give thanks to the Lord our God.
It is right to give our thanks and praise.

It is you, O Lord, who gives us rain and sun,
food and drink, day and night, work and rest,
friends and companions, today and eternity.

You crown your people with righteousness
by the gift of your Son, Jesus Christ,
whose life, death, resurrection, and ascension
rescues us and saves us for life eternal with you.

You come to us in our very breath
when we know our need and
when we cannot pray,
teaching us the words that raise us up.

With thanksgiving, we offer here what you have
    first given us.
Use us and these gifts for the sake of the life
    of the world. **Amen.**

CHARGE
Go in peace,
walk with the humble,
pray for your enemies,
live with thanksgiving.

BLESSING
May the strength of Almighty God surround you,
the mercy of the Lord Jesus Christ attend you,
and the peace of the Holy Spirit be yours,
today and always.

Questions for Reflection

What is prayer? When we hear the prayers of the two men in the temple
(Luke 18:9-14), what does Jesus' appreciation of the tax collector's prayer
tell us about the purpose of prayer?

Household Prayer: Morning

Living God,
you have made this day bright with the promise of your presence
as you crown each moment with hope.
Let your Holy Spirit pray in us now,

that in all our tasks—
at home, at work, at school, and in our community—
we may express the joy you have in us.
Be our peace, in Jesus' name. Amen.

Household Prayer: Evening

God of endings and beginnings,
who calls us to work and to rest,
we thank you for the joys and struggles of this day.
Teach us to come to a fuller knowledge of your will in our lives,
that each moment might be a sign of your love for us.
Take us now into your arms that in your safekeeping,
we may sleep and be renewed.
We pray this in Jesus' name. Amen.

Proper 26

(Sunday between October 30 and November 5 inclusive)
(if All Saints not observed on this day)

SEMICONTINUOUS

| Habakkuk 1:1–4; 2:1–4 | 2 Thessalonians 1:1–4, 11–12 |
| Psalm 119:137–144 | Luke 19:1–10 |

OPENING WORDS / CALL TO WORSHIP

Let all who are faithful offer prayers to God. *Ps. 32:6–7*
In times of distress, we will not be overwhelmed.
You are our hiding place, O Lord;
you preserve us from trouble
and surround us with glad cries of deliverance.

CALL TO CONFESSION

[Water is poured into the font.]
Even at our most faithful,
we stand in need of grace.
Because of God's unfailing love,
mercy is promised, even before we speak the truth.
In humility,
with confidence,
let us confess our sin before God and one another.

PRAYER OF CONFESSION

You are righteous, O God,
and your law is truth.
Yet we struggle to be faithful
and daily fail to live lives of justice and mercy.
[Silent prayers may be offered here.]
Forgive us again, O God;
keep covenant with us, as you have promised,
and soothe our aching souls,
through Jesus Christ, our Savior and Lord. Amen.

DECLARATION OF FORGIVENESS

[The presider plunges hands into the water and raises it up for all to see, saying:]

Because we have been buried with Christ
   in these waters,
we are raised to new life in him.
Forgiven and freed,
live lives worthy to your call,
and by the power of the Holy Spirit
seek to do good.

Rom. 6:4;
2 Thess. 1:11

PRAYER OF THE DAY

Gracious God,
in Jesus Christ you come to seek and
   save the lost.
You cover us with mercy
and uphold us in times of trouble.
Even when evil is all around,
you show us a vision of justice
and empower us with your own Spirit,
so that we do not lose hope.
All thanks and praise to you, O God,
for you come to save us and set us free.
In the name of Jesus we pray. **Amen.**

Hab. 2:3; Ps. 119:143;
Luke 19:10

PRAYER FOR ILLUMINATION

By your Spirit, O God,
let us hear you word,
that we may know your truth
and follow you with new resolve
to work and wait for the coming reign of Christ,
in whose name we pray. **Amen.**

PRAYERS OF INTERCESSION

We do not know how to pray,
but the Spirit intercedes for us
with sighs too deep for words.
Let us pray for the needs of the world, saying,
   Lord have mercy; hear our prayer.

Rom. 8:26

There is injustice at every turn, O Lord,
and evil surrounds us.
We pray for those in this country
and around the world
whose poverty is caused by the greed of others.
Lord have mercy; **hear our prayer.**

The earth has been gutted for ore;
its rivers are choked with filth.
The air we breathe causes our children and elders to fall ill.
Heal the earth, we pray, as you make us better stewards
of your good creation.
Lord have mercy; **hear our prayer.**

Your own beloved body is broken in pieces
and scarred by wounds that do not heal.
Instill your church with the desire to be whole,
and make us one with one another,
that we may worship you in unity.
Lord have mercy; **hear our prayer.**

Our cities are in despair, O God.
Violence and corruption are all around.
Protect us. Cleanse us. Heal us.
Provoke in us the desire for the common good,
for the sake of those who suffer the most.
Lord have mercy; **hear our prayer.**

So many we love are wracked by pain,
in body, mind, or spirit;
so many more we do not know
yearn for healing and care.
Pour out your healing spirit upon them,
and make us agents of your blessing.
Lord have mercy; **hear our prayer.**

For all those whose burdens are carried in secret,
and for our own needs, we pray . . . .
[A time of silence is kept.]
Lord have mercy; **hear our prayer.**

Our hearts, our hands, our voices are yours, O God.
Increase our faith, sustain our hope,
and send us out to do your work
and show your love.
In the name of Jesus Christ,
who is our all in all. **Amen.**

INVITATION TO THE OFFERING

Freely we have received;
freely may we give,
that those in need may see and touch and hear and eat
the grace of God in Jesus Christ.

PRAYER OF THANKSGIVING/DEDICATION

Lord, how can we thank you
for such wondrous love?
You have covered us with blessing
and sustained us with hope.
Most of all you have given us
your very self, for our life and the life of the world.
In gratitude we bring our gifts,
for the sake of those you love,
in Jesus' name. **Amen.**

CHARGE

Go in peace to love and serve the Lord.

BLESSING

May the grace of Christ attend you,
the love of God surround you,
and the Holy Spirit keep you,
this day and forevermore.

Questions for Reflection

The writer of Second Thessalonians "boast[s] of you among the churches of God for your steadfastness and faith during all your persecutions and the afflictions that you are enduring." How do Christians remain steadfast and faithful in the face of suffering? What sustains your hope, and how might you share that hope?

Household Prayer: Morning

With the morning light my hope is renewed,
and all my trust is in you, O God.
Lead me where you would have me go,
and show me what you would have me do,
to display your vision for the world to be
and, as far as I am able,
to live in accordance with your coming reign.
In the name of Jesus. Amen.

Household Prayer: Evening

The night is a gift from you, O God,
a time of repose for the weary.
Forgive any unfaithfulness in me,
and grant me peace,
that I may rest wholly in you. Amen.

Proper 26

(Sunday between October 30 and November 5 inclusive)
(if All Saints not observed on this day)

COMPLEMENTARY

Isaiah 1:10–18	2 Thessalonians 1:1–4, 11–12
Psalm 32:1–7	Luke 19:1–10

OPENING WORDS / CALL TO WORSHIP

We have gathered today in search of reformation.
We want to reform ourselves, our church,
  and our society.
We stand fearless at the edge of change.   *Ps. 46:2*
For God is in the midst of us and we
  shall not be moved.   *Ps. 46:5*
Be still, and know that God is God.   *Ps. 46:10*
God is our rock and our redeemer.   *Ps. 19:14*

CALL TO CONFESSION

When we keep our mistakes and misdeeds hidden away,   *Ps. 32:3, 5*
we are consumed with guilt and pain.
Therefore let us come into the light
and acknowledge our shortcomings,
trusting that God will forgive us and make us whole.

PRAYER OF CONFESSION

Loving God,   *Ps. 32:6–8*
you promise that all who faithfully confess to you
will be forgiven and preserved from trouble.
Trusting in your mercy,
we acknowledge the harm that we have done,
and the good we have failed to do.
Forgive us, we pray;
guide us in your truth, and teach us the way to go,
that we may love and serve you well.
In the name of Jesus we pray. Amen.

DECLARATION OF FORGIVENESS

Hear the good news: *Isa. 1:18;*
though your sins are like scarlet, they shall   *Ps. 32:10–11*
  be like snow.
For the Lord has promised to forgive all,
and to surround with steadfast love everyone
  who trusts in God.
In Jesus Christ, we are forgiven.

PRAYER OF THE DAY

You are our hiding place, O God;   *Ps. 32:7;*
you preserve us from trouble   *Luke 19:1–10*
and deliver us from death.
You teach us your wisdom
and show us your grace
by honoring the weak
and forgiving the wicked.
All glory and praise be to you,
for justice and mercy meet in you,
through Jesus Christ, in whose name we pray. **Amen.**

PRAYER FOR ILLUMINATION

God, through the power of your Holy Spirit,   *Luke 19:5*
open us to your Word
that we would hear what you would say to us today;
through Jesus Christ, who invites us to welcome
  him in,
even before we are ready or worthy. **Amen.**

PRAYERS OF INTERCESSION

God of Love and Justice,   *Isa. 1:14, 17;*
you have made it clear to us   *Ps. 32:7*
that you tire of our churchy words and
  religious festivals,
and that the worship you want from us
is an ethical life lived out in a society that we make just.
Hear our prayers for your whole creation, saying,
  God of justice, save your world.

We pray for the church and for all who live by faith,
doing charity and advocating for social change.
God of justice, **save your world.**

Cultivate peace between nations, between people,
and between political parties.
God of justice, **save your world.**

Protect and comfort those enduring the violence of
    war, or crime,
or the destructive forces of nature.
God of justice, **save your world.**

Preserve those who suffer violence at home and
    bullying at school,
and embolden those who see their trouble to help
    bring relief and help.
God justice, **save your world.**

Grant your healing mercies to those who are ill,
    or facing death,
and uphold those who care for them.
God of justice, **save your world.**

Delivering God, through Jesus Christ you come to us and
teach us the way of true worship:
doing good, seeking justice, rescuing the oppressed,
defending the orphan, and pleading for the widow.
Renew in us your vision of the worship that you want,
that we may take part in your work in the world,
by the power of your strengthening Spirit.
Through Jesus Christ we pray. **Amen.**

INVITATION TO THE OFFERING
In sharing ourselves we reflect God's vision   *Isa. 1:17*
of love and justice for the world.
Let us give freely,
so that the ministry of Jesus Christ may flourish
in this community and beyond.

PRAYER OF THANKSGIVING/DEDICATION

Holy One, we ask you to bless these tithes and offerings,
that our gifts may embody your vision of the kingdom
and bless those who are vulnerable, oppressed,
    and seeking justice;
in Jesus' name. **Amen.**

CHARGE

Learn to do good: seek justice, rescue the oppressed,
defend the orphan, plead for the widow,
trusting in the power of God to do all things.

BLESSING

Now may the deliverance of God,
the grace of Jesus Christ,
and the inspiration of the Holy Spirit
go with us all and give us peace.

Questions for Reflection

We sometimes imagine that we must earn God's love. In the story of
Zacchaeus, however, Jesus offered companionship to him even before
Zacchaeus made restoration to those he had cheated. Were the good works
of Zacchaeus the requirement or the response for receiving the love of
Jesus? What makes "grace" grace?

Household Prayer: Morning

Thank you, God, for this new day.
May I grow in faith
and increase in love,
that I may be worthy of the call you have placed on my life.
Let my words and my deeds
glorify the name of Jesus Christ,
that others may know of your grace
and abide in your love. Amen.

Household Prayer: Evening

God, thank you for the gift of this day.
I humbly ask you to forgive my shortcomings today,
having faith that you will forgive me.
Like Zacchaeus before me,
I thank Christ for coming home with me tonight and
assuring me that, no matter what, I am a child of God
and a member of your ecumenical community of faith.
I now take my rest, confident in your promise that
steadfast love surrounds those who trust in you. Amen.

All Saints

(November 1 or may be used first Sunday in November)

Daniel 7:1–3, 15–18   Ephesians 1:11–23
Psalm 149   Luke 6:20–31

OPENING WORDS / CALL TO WORSHIP
Sing to the Lord a new song!
Rejoice and give thanks,
for the Lord takes pleasure in the people.
Hallelujah!

CALL TO CONFESSION
For the peace and unity of the saints,
trusting in the promise of grace,
let us confess our sin to God and to one another.

PRAYER OF CONFESSION
God of the covenant,
who calls all people to reconciliation,
you have made us members of the very body of Christ;
yet we persist in wounding that body
with our divisions, our suspicions, and our neglect.
Forgive us, and teach us to nurture unity and peace.
For the sake of Jesus Christ
and the world he came to save; Amen.

DECLARATION OF FORGIVENESS
In the great compassion of our God,
the death and resurrection of Christ Jesus has shown us
God's forgiveness for our sins.
Therefore, I declare to you
the entire forgiveness for all your sins

in the name of the Father,
and of the Son,
and of the Holy Spirit. **Amen.**

PRAYER OF THE DAY

Holy God, who calls your people into one beloved community,
who teaches us the way of peace through life together,
who fills us with visions of your eternal reign:
as we now celebrate the communion of saints,
pour into our hearts the power of Christ,
who lives and reigns with you and the Holy Spirit,
one God, now and forever. **Amen.**

PRAYER FOR ILLUMINATION

Pour out your Spirit upon us, O God;
with your Word enlighten the eyes of our hearts,
that we might live in hope;
through Jesus Christ, our Lord. **Amen.**

PRAYERS OF INTERCESSION

Let us pray for the church, the world, and all in need, saying,
God, in your mercy, hear our prayer.

Author of all mercy, we give you thanks
for your goodness and loving-kindness to us
and to all whom you have made.
We praise you especially for your immeasurable love
in the redemption of the world by our Lord Jesus Christ,
for the means of grace,
and for hope in the ultimate reign of peace.
God, in your mercy, **hear our prayer.**

We pray for the holy church of God throughout the world,
for new congregations wherever they are gathered;
for missionaries, seminaries, preachers, and professors;
for musicians and artists; for architects and landscapers;
for funeral directors and those who care for cemeteries.

Make us generous toward our brothers and sisters
who live and breathe in your name.
  God, in your mercy, **hear our prayer.**

For those who wield earthly power,
for those who lead and those who follow,
that they may be moved by the image of your people,
disciples of Jesus, children of God,
diverse and sometimes in disagreement but living together
    in harmony,
a vision of the common good to which all nations
    might aspire.
  God, in your mercy, **hear our prayer.**

For those persecuted for the sake of righteousness and those
    weighed down by trial and distress,
that the example of the saints may give them courage
and the help of believers give them hope.
  God, in your mercy, **hear our prayer.**

For this assembly gathered to celebrate the Eucharist
in communion with the church in heaven and throughout
    the world,
that nourished by the word of truth and the bread of life,
we may bear witness in our own generation to the timeless
    gospel of Christ.
  God, in your mercy, **hear our prayer.**

For all who are in need:
for those who are in prison,
those awaiting trial,
those facing surgery,
all who lack medical help,
those who have no work,
those who work for too little pay,
the homeless,
and the ill.
  God, in your mercy, **hear our prayer.**

We give you thanks for those who have gone before us,
whose lives have shown us your truth,
and whose witness brought us and kept us in this community
of faith . . .
*[The names of those who have died in the past year may be spoken,
each followed by the tolling of a bell.]*
We trust in your never-failing love, O Lord,
joining your holy ones before the throne and the Lamb.
God, in your mercy, **hear our prayer.**

Into your hands, O Lord, we commend all for whom
we pray,
trusting that for these, and for us,
your care is constant and your heart is open;
through Jesus Christ, who lives and reigns with you and
the Holy Spirit,
one God, now and forever. **Amen.**

INVITATION TO THE OFFERING

With gratitude for God's blessings
through the power at work in Christ Jesus,
we gather now the gifts of the church
for the sake of the gospel.

PRAYER OF THANKSGIVING/DEDICATION

Holy One, all that we have comes from you.
You bless our lives with the companionship of your people,
the freedom that comes from forgiveness of sin,
the joy of thanksgiving for Earth and all its bounty.
Turn us toward those in need,
in the name of the one who gave himself for us,
Jesus Christ, our Savior. **Amen.**
[or]
Let us give thanks to the Lord our God.
It is right to give our thanks and praise.
We praise you, O God, that in the beginning
you turned darkness into light,
you made Earth and its creatures,
you provided all things for your good purposes.

You sent us Jesus who in word and deed
invited and admonished, taught and healed,
lifting up the poor and restoring the broken.
Through his eyes and on the cross we see our need.
In the empty tomb and his appearances to the saints,
we see our redemption.
By the Holy Spirit, our Advocate and guide,
we are shown the riches of our inheritance
and the power of the one who is the head over all things.
Lead us and guide us, O God, to use these gifts
for the sake of the life of the world;
through Jesus Christ we pray. **Amen.**

CHARGE

Love your enemies,
pray for those who oppose you,
answer evil with good,
gives to those in need;
for yours is the kingdom of God.

BLESSING

The God of our Lord Jesus Christ
give you a spirit of wisdom and revelation
to live in hope today and always.

Question for Reflection

Who are the saints that have accompanied you in the life of faith?

Household Prayer: Morning

God of blessing,
thank you for a new day to live for you.
In the company of all the saints
in heaven and on earth,
I rise to sing your praise.
Make me a worthy companion
of my ancestors in faith,
and let me love others
as I have been loved. Amen.

Household Prayer: Evening

Creator of the stars of night,
thank you for the gift of rest.
Forgive what wrong I have done today,
and heal any wounds I have caused.
Grant me, I pray, a peaceful rest,
that I may rise with the sun to serve you with joy. Amen.

Proper 27

(Sunday between November 6 and November 12 inclusive)

SEMICONTINUOUS

Haggai 1:15b–2:9	2 Thessalonians 2:1–5, 13–17
Psalm 145:1–5, 17–21	Luke 20:27–38
or Psalm 98	

OPENING WORDS / CALL TO WORSHIP

Make a joyful noise to the Lord, all the earth;   *Ps. 98:4–6*
break forth into joyous song and sing praises.
Sing praises to the Lord with the lyre,
with the lyre and the sound of melody.
With trumpets and the sound of the horn
make a joyful noise before the King, the Lord.
Come, make a joyful noise, sing praises!
    Come, let us worship the Lord!

CALL TO CONFESSION

The psalmist assures us that the Lord is near   *Ps. 145:18*
to all who call on God in truth.
So with that assurance of God's presence,
God's steadfast love,
and God's overwhelming mercy,
let us confess our sins before God and one another.

PRAYER OF CONFESSION

Holy God we come before you a broken people in a broken world.
We confess we have ignored, yet again, your assured presence.
We have forged our own paths and charted our own waters.
In the name of independence we have ignored your aid,
    your comfort, and your peace.
We have called upon you in desperation
rather than recalling your mighty and faithful acts in all times
    and places.

Forgive us.
You have been with us in exile and liberation;
be with us even now. Amen.

DECLARATION OF FORGIVENESS

The psalmist declares that God hears the cry
of the beloved   *Ps. 145:19, 21*
and saves them.
Be assured: in Jesus Christ, we are forgiven.
Praise the Lord, and bless God's holy name forever.

PRAYER OF THE DAY

Holy God,
you have commanded us to not be afraid
and assured us of your presence.
In the midst of trials and joys,
sorrows and dreams
may we know your presence and rejoice.
Grant us courage, O God,
to take delight in your spirit in all times and all places.
Grant us faith, O God,
to see the myriad of ways you give life.
Grant us hope, O God,
to participate in your work in the world.
Grant us love, O God,
to welcome, respond, and act with compassion in all
we say and do.
In the name of Jesus Christ, we pray. **Amen.**

PRAYER FOR ILLUMINATION

God of wisdom,
by your Spirit may your Word be proclaimed,
that we may know good news in our hearts and minds
and bear witness to the glory of our Lord Jesus Christ
in word and deed.
Quiet in us any voice but your own,
that we might hear your Word to us today. **Amen.**

PRAYERS OF INTERCESSION

Holy God your loving-kindness knows no ending.   *Hag. 2:5*
Out of the depths of slavery you heard the cry of
      your people
and responded with liberation.
Hear us from the depths of our captivity.

For your people held captive by addictions that ravage body,
      mind, and spirit we affirm:
your Spirit abides among us, we will not fear.

For your people held captive by violence, abuse, and
      exploitation we attest:
your Spirit abides among us, we will not fear.

For your people held captive by illness, weakness, and
      vulnerability we recall:
your Spirit abides among us, we will not fear.

For your people held captive by economic or
      vocational poverty we proclaim:
your Spirit abides among us, we will not fear.

Holy God your loving-kindness knows no ending.
Hear our prayers and keep us faithful
until the coming of our Lord Jesus Christ,
in whose name we pray. **Amen.**

INVITATION TO THE OFFERING

In celebration of the God of life
who sustains, upholds, saves, and watches over us,
let us continue our worship
through the offering of our gifts, tithes, and offerings
      to almighty God.

PRAYER OF THANKSGIVING/DEDICATION

For the gifts offered this day and every day
we give thanks, O God.
Make us good stewards of all you have entrusted to our care.

May these gifts be used to serve your beloved creation,
to sustain your children in all they say and do,
and to build up your kingdom throughout the earth.

CHARGE

Go into the world in peace,   *2 Thess. 2:15*
bearing witness to the God of presence.
Bless God's holy name forever and ever,
and hold fast to the traditions you have been taught,
giving thanks in all things.

BLESSING

And now may our Lord Jesus Christ himself   *2 Thess. 2:16–17*
and God our Creator, by the power of the Holy Spirit,
who loved us and through grace gave us eternal comfort
     and good hope,
comfort your hearts and strengthen them in every
     good work and word,
this day and ever more.

Questions for Reflection

How will it change the way we treat one another—or even ourselves—if,
like the psalmist declares, we bless God's name every day rather than cling
to the negative or complain about the things that do not go as planned?

The writer of second Thessalonians implores his readers to "hold fast to the
traditions that you were taught by us, either by word of mouth or by our
letter" (2 Thess. 2:15). Identify some traditions you should hold on to. Are
there traditions we should reclaim? What about traditions that have served
their purpose and can be let go? What are the traditions of the church?

Household Prayer: Morning

God of life,
for this new day we give thanks.
May we bear witness to the gift of life in all we say and do,
from the flowers that bloom to the critters that creep,
from the friends we seek out to the strangers we encounter.
As the birds sing out their praises, may we, too, make a joyful noise.

May our words and our actions reveal your good news.
Help us to be inspired and awed by your extraordinary creation. Amen.

Household Prayer: Evening

Holy God,
you have indeed done marvelous things and we give thanks.
Throughout this day we were challenged and found hope;
we were surprised by the places and people who give witness to you.
Be with us and those we love this night.
Comfort those who are uneasy or afraid.
Guide us through the night to the dawn of a new day
filled with hope and promise. Amen.

Proper 27

(Sunday between November 6 and November 12 inclusive)

COMPLEMENTARY

Job 19:23–27a	2 Thessalonians 2:1–5, 13–17
Psalm 17:1–9	Luke 20:27–38

OPENING WORDS / CALL TO WORSHIP

God chose you as the first fruits of salvation,   *2 Thess. 2:13*
calling you to receive the good news of Jesus Christ.
Thanks be to God for such extravagant grace!
Praise the Lord!

CALL TO CONFESSION

The psalmist tells us that the Lord is near   *Ps. 145:18*
to all who call on God in truth.
Therefore let us now turn to God in prayer,
trusting in the nearness and compassion of the Holy One.

PRAYER OF CONFESSION

Gracious God, we call upon you, for you will answer us.   *Ps. 17:3–8*
We confess that we have transgressed in our speech
and have not always avoided the ways of the violent.
Our steps have not always held to your paths.
Try us, forgive us, and heal us, dear God.
Set us on your right ways, and guard us as the apple
    of your eye,
embracing us once more in your steadfast love. Amen.

DECLARATION OF FORGIVENESS

Through grace Christ gives us   *2 Thess. 2:16*
eternal comfort and good hope.
I declare to you, in the name of Jesus Christ,
you are forgiven.

PRAYER OF THE DAY

Ever-Living God, splendid and wondrous   *Ps. 145:2–3, 5, 20;*
     are your acts!   *2 Thess. 2:17*
You give life and breath to your whole creation
and watch over those you love.
Strengthen us in every good work,
and keep us in your care,
that our days may be long to bless you and praise you.
You are great, and greatly to be praised! **Amen.**

PRAYER FOR ILLUMINATION

Redeeming God, through the power of your Holy Spirit,   *Job 19:25*
connect us to eternity through our hearing of your Word,
that we might know your living presence
and seek to do your will;
in Jesus' name. **Amen.**

PRAYERS OF INTERCESSION

God of the Living and the Dead, we are forever
     living to you.   *Luke 20:38*
You call us to be the body of the risen Christ,   *1 Cor. 12:37*
extending eternal comfort and good hope to those
     all around us.   *2 Thess. 2:16*
Lord, you are just in all your ways and kind
     in all your doings.   *Ps. 145:17*
We pray for the church universal and for all who bring
     comfort and hope to others.
Lord, you are just in all your ways and kind
     in all your doings.
We pray for peace between nations, between religions
     and denominations,
and between families and among all people.
Lord, you are just in all your ways and kind
     in all your doings.
We pray with thanksgiving for all the guides and mentors
     who have gone before us
and for those who declare your mighty acts from
     one generation to the next.   *Ps. 145:4*
Lord, you are just in all your ways and kind
     in all your doings.

We pray for those who suffer violence and for those
who inflict it,
that they may hold fast to your paths. *Ps. 17:4–5*
**Lord, you are just in all your ways and kind
in all your doings.**
We pray for those who are nearing death, that they
may know their redeemer lives. *Job 19:25*
**Lord, you are just in all your ways and kind
in all your doings.**
Redeeming God, through Jesus Christ you strengthen
us and give us hope. *2 Thess. 2:16*
Renew our hearts that we may worship and
bless you forever, *Ps. 145:1*
eternally making joyful noise and singing new songs *Ps. 98:4*
to proclaim the good news of your grace. **Amen.**

INVITATION TO THE OFFERING
In many and various ways, God gives us
comfort and hope, *2 Thess. 2:16*
even the hope of eternal life.
In gratitude, then, let us give generously.

PRAYER OF THANKSGIVING/DEDICATION
Holy One, in gratitude for all that you give us,
including those who have gone before us,
we offer you these gifts and ask you to bless
and multiply them,
that they may become the good work and word *2 Thess. 2:17*
that comforts and strengthens both our hearts
and the hearts of others. **Amen.** *2 Thess. 2:17*

CHARGE
Stand firm and hold fast *2 Thess. 2:15*
to the grace you have received.

BLESSING
Now may our Lord Jesus Christ himself,
and God our parent,
who loves us and, through grace,
gives us eternal comfort and good hope,

comfort your hearts and strengthen them
in every good deed and word.   *2 Thess. 2:16–17*

Questions for Reflection

We each have our own ideas and visions of what happens to us after we
die. When the opponents of Jesus tried to trick him by asking a convoluted
question about what heaven is like after we die, Jesus replied by saying that
God is not the God of the dead but of the living because we are always
alive to God (Luke 20:38). How does that inform our sense of Christian
community, of the communion of saints, and of life everlasting?

Household Prayer: Morning

Holy One, I want to see you today in this world with my own eyes.
Even though your greatness is unsearchable,
today I want to meditate on your wondrous works all around me.
Give me the eyes of faith through which to see you.
Renew me, that I may praise you with a new song. Amen.

Household Prayer: Evening

God, thank you for guiding my steps on your paths today.
Where my feet may have slipped, forgive me.
You have wondrously shown me your steadfast love through the course
    of this day.
Now let me fall asleep in the shadow of your wings,
for I have seen today that you are my redeemer, the living God. Amen.

Proper 28

(Sunday between November 13 and November 19 inclusive)

SEMICONTINUOUS

Isaiah 65:17–25	2 Thessalonians 3:6–13
Isaiah 12	Luke 21:5–19

OPENING WORDS / CALL TO WORSHIP

Sing praises to the Lord, for God has done gloriously; *Isa. 12:5–6*
let us sing God's praises throughout all the earth.
Shout aloud and sing for joy,
from the highest peaks, to the deepest caverns.
Shout aloud and sing for joy,
from the tiniest creatures, to the greatest herds.
Shout aloud and sing for joy,
in the midst of our joys and our sorrows.
Shout aloud and sing for joy, as we come to worship
   the God of all creation!

CALL TO CONFESSION

Just as the prophet Isaiah assured God's people
   so many years ago *Isa. 12:2–3*
he assures us now that God is our salvation.
It is because of that confidence,
because of that promise,
that we dare approach God with our confession.

PRAYER OF CONFESSION

God of peace we confess we are a people of fear.
We have let anxiety rule our days and worry our nights.
We have been distracted by nerves and focused on tension.
We confess we have ignored your command to not be afraid.
Forgive us, O God.
Calm our hearts, settle our stomachs,
and renew in us the ability to find our comfort in you. Amen.

DECLARATION OF FORGIVENESS

The prophet Isaiah assures us: *Isa. 65:17–18*
God is building a new heaven and a new earth;
the former things will not be remembered
> or come to mind.
Forgiven and freed,
rejoice in what the Lord is creating in you,
> in me, in all creation.

PRAYER OF THE DAY

God, who labored creation into being,
we give thanks for this day and the privilege to work in your world.
We pray this day for those for whom this Lord's Day is not a day
> of rest but of toil.
We pray this day for those who cannot afford to take Sabbath
and for those who believe they cannot afford to take Sabbath.
Grant us the strength to labor for what is right, just, and fair.
Grant us the wisdom to speak out for those who are enslaved,
> oppressed, and exploited.
Grant us the ability to break the chains of injustice and hear the
> voices of people long silenced.
We pray this day for the privilege to work in your world;
may we make it better.
In Jesus' name we pray. **Amen.**

PRAYER FOR ILLUMINATION

God of the earthquake and the silence,
quiet in us any voice but your own,
that by the power of the Holy Spirit we might hear,
and in hearing we might believe,
and in believing we might act,
making way for your new creation. **Amen.**

PRAYERS OF INTERCESSION

[A brief silence may be kept after each intercession.]
God of new beginnings   *Isa. 65:19–25*
You have promised us a season
in which weeping will no longer be heard,
nor cries of distress.
Yet we live in a season filled with weeping and distress.

This day we come before you offering prayers for those
    who weep with grief:
for those who mourn the death of loved ones;
the loss of employment;
the pain of transition.

This day we come before you offering prayers for those
    who cry out in distress:
for the rumblings of hungry bellies;
the lament of the addict;
the pleas of the homeless.

This day we come before you offering prayers for those
    who labor in vain:
for those enslaved in fields, factories, and mines;
for those whose work cripples their bodies and their spirits;
for those who toil without recognition, wage, or honor.
You have promised us a season of blessing.

You have promised us a season of peace.
We pray for the coming of that holy time throughout
    your beloved creation,
for the sake of your beloved Son, and our Savior,
    Jesus Christ. **Amen.**

INVITATION TO THE OFFERING
In a world filled with blessings
we celebrate our privilege and our responsibility
to share those blessings.
Let us celebrate the God of overwhelming blessings
by continuing our worship
through the offering of our tithes and gifts.

PRAYER OF THANKSGIVING/DEDICATION
God of the wolf and the lamb, the lion and the ox,   *Isa. 65:17, 25*
we give thanks for these gifts
and pray they might be agents of your peace.
May they serve your creation
as we seek your new heaven and new earth.

Help us take these gifts out into a world
filled with distress and calm it.
Help us take these gifts out into a world
filled with pain and heal it.
Help us take these gifts out into a world
filled with silence and speak up;
In Jesus' name. **Amen.**

CHARGE

Go out into the world in peace.   *Isa. 65:21–25*
Live fully.
Build homes.
Plant vineyards.
Give thanks.
Work for what is right.

BLESSING

And now may the God of our salvation,
our strength and our comfort,
guard your hearts and minds
this day and evermore.

Questions for Reflection

In a world that values busyness above all else, how do we, in a healthy
and faithful way, hold Paul's demand to work well with the command for
Sabbath? "Brothers and sisters, do not be weary in doing what is right"
(2 Thess. 3:13). Even Paul realizes that it can become tedious to work
for justice. What are ways that we might stay energized in a seemingly
impossible task? Jesus' words in Luke are particularly challenging; he
assures his disciples and believers that they will be persecuted, handed
over, betrayed, and hated (Luke 21:12–19). Where is there good news in a
text filled with such scary assurances?

Household Prayer: Morning

God of comfort,
we give thanks for the dawning of a new day.
Even though we have turned from you
you have reached for us.

Even though we have been afraid
you have been our strength and our might.
May we draw life-giving water with joy this day,
giving thanks for the multitude of gifts and challenges we face,
singing praises to the Lord throughout all the earth. Amen.

Household Prayer: Evening

God of salvation,
we are reminded of the myriad of ways
you have strengthened and supported us today.
In the midst of challenge and promise
you reach for us.
You create a new heaven and a new earth
and call us to participate in the renewing of hearts and minds.
Be with us and those we love this night.
Be with your beloved whose fear prevails over your comfort,
and bring us through this night
to the dawning of a new day. Amen.

Proper 28

(Sunday between November 13 and November 19 inclusive)

COMPLEMENTARY

Malachi 4:1–2a	2 Thessalonians 3:6–13
Psalm 98	Luke 21:5–19

OPENING WORDS / CALL TO WORSHIP
Make a joyful noise to the Lord, all the earth!
Sing to the Lord a new song, for God has done
marvelous things.   *Ps. 98*

CALL TO CONFESSION
Trusting in God's goodness to us,
let us confess our sin before God and one another.

PRAYER OF CONFESSION
God of Mercy,   *2 Thess. 3:6-13*
we confess that we have not been obedient sons
and daughters.
We have grown idle in the work of discipleship
and weary in doing what is right.
We have been selfish in our actions and insistent
in claiming our rights.
We have not honored the tradition of the apostles,
or imitated the example of your saints.
Forgive us, we pray.
Show us the way of repentance,
free us from our idle ways,
and strengthen us to be faithful disciples of
Jesus Christ,
through whom we pray. Amen.

DECLARATION OF FORGIVENESS

Hear the good news:
Christ is merciful to all who turn to him in repentance.
In the name of Jesus Christ,
we are forgiven.

PRAYER OF THE DAY

O God, our Redeemer,
all creation sings your praise!
You are justice and mercy,
judgment and grace.
Following our Lord Jesus Christ,
we seek to be faithful,
ever sustained by your Spirit,
that we might stand blameless at the last
with Christ, in whose name we pray. **Amen.**

PRAYER FOR ILLUMINATION

Almighty God,   *2 Thess. 3:13*
as the Scriptures are read and your Word proclaimed,
reveal to us the way of salvation
by the power of your Holy Spirit,
that we may not grow weary in doing what is right. **Amen.**

PRAYERS OF INTERCESSION

In peace, let us pray to the Lord, saying,   *Isa. 12:2;*
    hear our prayer.   *Luke 25:13–15*

Merciful God, our salvation in whom we trust,
you who are eternal,
know our daily joys and sorrows
and give us grace to bring our needs before you.
We pray for pastors, teachers, *[bishops, etc.]*
and all the saints who lead your church.
Inspire them by your Holy Spirit
and help the church's faithful to uphold them.
God in your mercy, **hear our prayer.**

We pray for elected officials and for civil servants.
Stir them to heed justice
and rouse the church to hold them accountable.
God in your mercy, **hear our prayer.**

We pray for those who are sick or in trouble, especially *N.*
Comfort them with grace
and empower your church to minister to them.
God in your mercy, **hear our prayer.**

We pray for all who suffer the violence
of human hands or natural disaster, especially *N.*
Shield them with your holy angels
and motivate your church to care for them.
God in your mercy, **hear our prayer.**

We pray for children and for the defenseless.
Protect them with your care
and strengthen your church to tend to them.
God in your mercy, **hear our prayer.**

We pray for all those who may live in fear of your judgment,
who have known rejection,
or who live on the margins of society.
Show them the love that casts out fear
and enable them to find a place in your church,
that we may be a community of reconciliation.
God in your mercy, **hear our prayer.**

We pray for our enemies.
Empower the church to love them
and to look for a day when we may live together
in your reconciling love.
God in your mercy, **hear our prayer.**

We pray for all those who suffer for the name of Christ.
Let your people in every place
be ready to offer testimony to the gospel
and bear persecution with the confidence in your truth.
God in your mercy, **hear our prayer.**

God of mercy, our strength and our might,
receive these prayers, which we offer trusting in your goodness.
We ask in weakness according to our need,
but you give wisely according to your gracious care for all the world.
Therefore, we pray in gratitude and in hope,
through our Savior, Jesus Christ. **Amen.**

INVITATION TO THE OFFERING
Let us offer ourselves and our gifts to God,
with gratitude and praise.

PRAYER OF THANKSGIVING/DEDICATION
Loving God,
before we give to you, you have given to us.
All we offer we have received from you.
We thank you for your goodness,
and we praise you for your bountiful works,
though Christ by the power of the Holy Spirit. **Amen.**

CHARGE
Be strong in the truth of God.
Bear witness to the gospel.
Persevere in the face of evil.
Persist in your commitment to Christ.
Live without fear.
Love without reserve.

BLESSING
May the grace of God,
the love of Christ,
and the power of the Holy Spirit be with you always.

Questions for Reflection

Jesus speaks of wars, insurrections, earthquakes, famines, and plagues, but instructs his followers, "Do not be terrified!" How does our witness to the gospel include resistance to our natural impulse to be terrorized by evil? Have you ever suffered persecution as a Christian because you refused to go along with social pressure to be fearful of enemies, terrorists, criminals, illegal aliens, or other pariahs?

Household Prayer: Morning

Lord of Creation, every morning you renew the earth with light.
I praise for you the morning light, and I rejoice in the life you
    have given me.
Let me be a friend to those who do not know your love.
Let me offer hope to those who do not trust your goodness.
Let me embody graciousness to those who do not understand your peace.
Help me to be a blessing to all I encounter—
to bear witness to your goodness through Jesus Christ. Amen.

Household Prayer: Evening

Surely God is my salvation;   *Isa. 12:2*
I will trust and will not be afraid.
For the Lord God is my strength and my might;
he has become my salvation.

Lord, the day is done and my labors must end.
I trust to your care all that I have done
and all that I have left undone,
for you alone are my strength.
Give me peaceful rest
that I may raise to faithful service,
with Jesus Christ my Lord. Amen.

Reign of Christ / Proper 29

SEMICONTINUOUS

Jeremiah 23:1–6	Colossians 1:11–20
Luke 1:68-79	Luke 23:33–43

OPENING WORDS / CALL TO WORSHIP

Blessed be the Lord God of Israel,   *Luke 1:68*
for God has looked favorably on God's people and
   redeemed them.
Blessed be the Lord God of Israel,
for God has called us God's own beloved and called
   each of us by name.
Blessed be the Lord God of Israel,
for God has blessed God's creation and called us to worship.
Blessed be the Lord God of Israel!

CALL TO CONFESSION

We do not confess our sins in the *hope* of forgiveness;   *Col. 1:13–14*
we confess our sins with the *certainty* of forgiveness.
For the apostle Paul assures us
that we have been rescued from the power of darkness,
and transferred into the kingdom of God's beloved son,
in whom we have redemption, the forgiveness of sins.
And so with that promise, that assurance, that redemption
we confess our sins before God and one another.

PRAYER OF CONFESSION

Holy God,
we confess that we have neglected to declare Jesus
the king and model for our lives.
We have been quick to call on others
to follow the ways of Christ
yet slow to do the same.

We have been bold in demanding generosity,
mercy, and forgiveness
yet quiet when it comes to offering inclusion,
love, and compassion.
Forgive us, O God.
Restore in us, yet again, the commitment to
be more Christlike
in word, in deed, and in spirit. Amen.

DECLARATION OF FORGIVENESS

All things, in heaven and on earth,   *Col. 1:20*
are reconciled to God in Jesus Christ.
Forgiveness is ours through faith in the Lord,
in whom God was pleased to dwell.
Know that you are forgiven, and be at peace.

PRAYER OF THE DAY

God of all times and all places,
be with us in this time and this place.
Just as you have spoken to your people
through prophets and poets,
we pray that we might hear the Word
you speak to us today.
Just as you have spoken to your people through
deeds and miracles,
we pray that we might have eyes
to see the Word you speak to us today.
Just as you have called your people
to act in the midst of your creation,
we pray that we might have feet to walk
and hands to reach out;
for the sake of your Son, in whose name we pray. **Amen.**

PRAYER FOR ILLUMINATION

Holy God,
through the generations you have spoken to us.
You have sent voices crying out in the wilderness.
You have sent the words of an overjoyed new father and
an expectant mother.
You have sent the assurance of a condemned man on a cross.

Quiet in us any voice but your own
that, by the power of your Spirit,
we might hear the words you speak to us today. **Amen.**

PRAYERS OF INTERCESSION
Loving God, *Jer. 23:5–6*
you have assured us that the days are surely coming
when your people will know peace,
your people will know justice,
your people will know righteousness.
Confident in your promises, we proclaim with faith:
The Lord is our righteousness.

You have assured us that a leader
will come to rule with wisdom.
We pray this day for those in particular need
of justice, righteousness, and mercy.
We pray for the trampled, the ignored, the brushed aside.
We pray for the home-less, the love-less, and the health-less.
We pray for leaders in governments, homes,
communities, and schools,
that they may know the influence of wisdom rather than power;
and declare with faith:
The Lord is our righteousness.

You have assured us of the salvation and safety of your people.
We pray this day for those who only know violence:
those whose countries have been torn apart by invasion, civil war,
    and private armies,
those whose communities have been forgotten by all but the
    warlords and gangs,
those whose homes are places of danger and fear rather than
    sanctuary and love.
May they declare with certitude:
The Lord is our righteousness.

God of all creation we pray this day for the reign of Jesus the Christ.
We pray that in the midst of chaos we might hear Jesus' word to us;
that in the midst of heartache we might know Jesus' presence,
and in the midst of a cacophony of voices we might proclaim:
The Lord is our righteousness. **Amen.**

INVITATION TO THE OFFERING

The blessed apostle Paul *Col. 1:15–16*
sings the praises of our Lord Jesus Christ,
the firstborn of all creation;
in whom all things in heaven and on earth were created.
Let us affirm God's sovereignty over all creation,
continuing our worship
through the offering of our gifts to the Lord.

PRAYER OF THANKSGIVING/DEDICATION

Holy God,
you have looked upon your people with mercy, generosity,
and love.
You have granted your favor to your people,
offering them redemption, salvation, and wisdom.
And so we offer these gifts
for your hurting and broken world.
May they be multiplied to do your service.
May we be strengthened to do your work.
In the name of Jesus the Christ,
who multiplied small gifts and fed multitudes. **Amen.**

CHARGE

Go out into the world in peace, *Luke 1:79*
declaring Christ the king and ruler over all creation.
Go out into the world with courage,
supporting the ways he gives light to those who sit
in darkness
and guides our feet in the way of peace.

BLESSING

And now may the holy triune God, *Col. 1:15*
the visible and invisible,
guide your feet,
strengthen your hands,
and fortify your heart this day and evermore.
In the name of the Creator, Sustainer, and Redeemer.

Questions for Reflection

The prophet Jeremiah warns of shepherds who will destroy and scatter God's people (Jer. 23:1–2). How do we discern the difference between shepherds who have come to scatter and shepherds who have been raised up by God? How do the stories of Zechariah's prophecy and Jesus' crucifixion affirm the ways we declare the kingship of Jesus? Paul declares that peace was made through the blood of the cross (Col. 1:20). How do we think about the inherent violence in the crucifixion? Is there a way to reconcile the call to be peacemakers with this statement that peace comes through the blood of the cross?

Household Prayer: Morning

God of the new day,
at the dawning of the first day
you spoke creation into being and declared it good.
You crafted each flower and vegetable
and bird of the air and beast of the land,
and there at all of it was Jesus the Christ.
We give thanks for the dawning of this day
and pray we might know your holy triune presence
in all we see and do.
Guard our hearts, minds, spirits, and bodies
that we, too, might sing the goodness of creation
and remember your call to be good stewards of it all. Amen.

Household Prayer: Evening

Ever-present God,
even on that dark day, in that dark place called the Skull,
you were present to the suffering and those in pain.
Be present to the suffering on this night, too,
and rain down mercy and justice upon your beloved creation.
Be with us and those we love this night,
and bring us through to the dawning of a new day
filled with righteousness, love, and peace. Amen.

Reign of Christ / Proper 29

Jeremiah 23:1–6   Colossians 1:11–20
Psalm 46   Luke 23:33–43

OPENING WORDS / CALL TO WORSHIP
Worship Christ, Eternal Son of God;
honor Christ, Incarnate Son of Mary;
serve Christ, Glorious Ruler of creation;
for to Christ belong the power and the glory of the Almighty.
Praise be to God.

CALL TO CONFESSION
With humble hearts,
trusting in grace,
let us confess our sins before God and one another.

PRAYER OF CONFESSION
Almighty God,
you brought forth the world for the love of Christ,
yet we have lived in rebellion and turned away from
   our created purpose.
We have acknowledged the Lordship of Christ with our lips,
but we have not honored him with our lives.
We have served the idols of wealth and privilege;
we have sought the protection of violence to oppose violence;
we have lived in fear of death and loss;
we have not loved our neighbors, nor sought reconciliation
   with our enemies.
Therefore we pray:
Break our rebellious will.

Instruct our hearts in the ways of peace.
Expose our insincere thoughts.
Give us integrity in our quest for truth.
Release us from the fear of death.
Grant us courage in the face of evil.
Free us for joyful service in Christ our Lord.
Empower us to live as citizens of your kingdom.
For the sake of the world, in the name of Christ. **Amen.**

DECLARATION OF FORGIVENESS

God has rescued us for the power of darkness
and transferred us into the kingdom of the
beloved Son,
in whom we have redemption, the forgiveness
of sins.
Through Christ our Lord, we are forgiven.

Col. 1:13-14

PRAYER OF THE DAY

Almighty God,
through the Lordship of your Son, Jesus Christ,
the powers and dominions of the world obtain
their purpose,
and creation finds its meaning.
Reveal to the world the gracious rule of Christ,
end all enmity among the nations,
and bring us soon to his glorious, peaceable kingdom;
through Christ who lives and reigns with you and
the Holy Spirit,
one God, forever and ever. **Amen.**

Col. 1:16–17

PRAYER FOR ILLUMINATION

Lord, open our hearts to receive your Word;
by your Spirit free us from the power of darkness
and show to us the inheritance of the saints of light. **Amen.**

Col. 1:12–13

PRAYERS OF INTERCESSION

From the Cross Jesus prayed to God,
"Father, forgive them; for they do not know what
they are doing."

Luke 23:34

Let us pray for our world that does not know the
    forgiveness of God
and does not consider the Lordship of Christ, saying,
Let your Kingdom come.

For the rulers, dominions, and powers of the world
who exercise authority over human communities,
that they may repent of war, renounce oppression,
and serve the common good,
let us pray to the Lord: **Let your kingdom come.**

For the planet Earth that God has given to humankind as our home,
that we may be good and wise stewards of its resources,
and that those with the power to exploit its bounty
may restrain the desire for selfish gain,
let us pray to the Lord: **Let your kingdom come.**

For the church universal,
that all who are baptized in Christ
may bear witness to his glorious reign
and serve him in the world,
let us pray to the Lord: **Let your kingdom come.**

For our enemies,
that we may love them in the way of Jesus,
let us pray to the Lord: **Let your kingdom come.**

For our friends and neighbors,
that we may we may dwell with them in peace,
let us pray to the Lord: **Let your kingdom come.**

For those whose bodies are under the demonic reign of addiction,
that the power of their addiction may be broken
and that they may be free to receive the gentle rule of Christ,
let us pray to the Lord: **Let your kingdom come.**

Almighty God,
hear the prayers of your people for the sake of our world.
Let our prayers be confirmed in our lives,
that we may bear witness to the Lordship of Jesus,
through whom we pray. **Amen.**

INVITATION TO THE OFFERING
With gratitude, let us offer ourselves and our gifts to God.

PRAYER OF THANKSGIVING/DEDICATION
Almighty God,   *Col. 1:18*
receive our offering for the sake of Christ our Lord.
Make us worthy stewards of your gifts
and generous citizens of the kingdom of your Son, Jesus Christ,
through whom we pray. **Amen.**

CHARGE
Worship Christ, Eternal Son of God.
Honor Christ, Incarnate Son of Mary.
Serve Christ, Glorious Ruler of creation.

BLESSING
May the blessing of God, holy Trinity, be with you,
this day and forevermore.

Question for Reflection

Jesus asks God to forgive those who crucified him, saying, "Father, forgive them; for they do not know what they are doing." What does it mean to offer forgiveness to others before they are aware of their offense?

Household Prayer: Morning

Lord Jesus, remember me when you come into your kingdom
and enable me to live today for the attainment of paradise,
that as far as I am able
I may be a sign of God's kingdom. Amen.

Lord Jesus, if I have not honored you with all my heart,
forgive me.
If I have offended out of ignorance,
pardon me.
Let me sleep in peace
and rise with a renewed dedication to serve you. Amen.

❧ ADDITIONAL RESOURCES ☙

Greetings

It is appropriate to begin each service with a greeting quoted or drawn from Scripture. You may choose to use the same greeting for several weeks or throughout a season.

Grace and peace in Jesus Christ our Lord.
Amen.

The Lord is our light and our salvation.   *Ps. 27:1*
Thanks be to God.

Grace to you and peace from God our Father   *2 Thess. 1:2*
and the Lord Jesus Christ.

Grace and peace from the One God
who comes to us as
Lover, the Beloved, and Love itself.

The grace of our Lord Jesus Christ,
the love of God,
and the communion of the Holy Spirit
be with you all.
And also with you.

Blessed be the triune God
who created all things,
who renews and sustains us,

who pours out upon us
the fullness of peace.
Amen.

The grace and mercy of the Blessed Trinity,
One God,
maker, redeemer, and sustainer of all things,
be with you all.
And also with you.

Thanksgiving for Baptism

[at the font]
The Lord be with you.
And also with you.
Let us give thanks to the Lord our God.
It is right to give our thanks and praise.
Holy God, we give you thanks and praise
for the life-sustaining gift of water:
At the dawn of creation
your Spirit swept across the swirling of the deep;
in the days of Noah
you washed away all evil from the face of the earth;
in the time of Moses
you led your people through the surging sea into freedom;
by the rivers of Babylon
you heard our cry and brought us home at last;
in the waters of the Jordan
Jesus was baptized by John and anointed with your Spirit.

[touching the water]
We give thanks for the water of baptism,
in which you deliver us from captivity to sin
and by which we share in Christ's saving death
and live-giving resurrection.
Pour out your Holy Spirit among us now.
Refresh us, renew us, restore us by your grace
so that we may live faithfully as the beloved people
you have chosen, called, and claimed in Christ Jesus.

All praise and honor and glory are yours,
O Triune God, now and forever. **Amen.**

[lifting water from the font]
Remember your baptism and be thankful.

[making the sign of the cross over the people]
In the name of the Father,
and of the Son,
and of the Holy Spirit. **Amen.**

Great Prayers of Thanksgiving / Eucharistic Prayers

These prayers are offered as supplementary resources that are intended to be in line with approved and published denominational worship materials. They may be adapted for your congregational context.

GENERAL USE

The Lord be with you.
And also with you.
Lift up your hearts.
We lift them to the Lord.
Let us give thanks to the Lord our God.
It is right to give our thanks and praise.

It is right, it is good, and it is joyful
to give thanks to you, God of mystery and miracle.

When there was only darkness,
    you made light.
When we cried out to you from captivity,
    you claimed us as your own.
When we forgot our love for you,
    you did not forget us,
sending your prophets to turn us around and
renewing your promises
    with a bow in the sky,
    the parting of the sea,
    your own Son.

And so we praise you,
tuning our voices to the angels' songs,
joining all those who sing on earth and in heaven:

Holy, holy, holy, Lord, God of power and might,
heaven and earth are full of your glory.
Hosanna in the highest.

Blessed is the One who comes in the name of the Lord.
Hosanna in the highest.

Thank you for Jesus—
for his teaching and healing,
his challenging and feeding,
his living and dying and rising,
that we might be raised with him,
and all the world made new.

We thank you that on the night before he died
he took bread, gave thanks, and broke it,
and shared it with his friends,
saying, take, eat—my body broken for you.
Thank you for the way he took the cup,
the new covenant sealed in his blood,
shed for the forgiveness of sins.
Whenever you eat and drink, he said,
do it in remembrance of me.

With thanksgiving we take this bread and wine,
gifts of the good earth,
offering ourselves as a living sacrifice
dedicated to your service.

Dying, you destroyed our death;
rising, you restored our life.
Lord Jesus, come in glory.

Pour out your Holy Spirit on your people gathered here
    and on these gifts—
        bread and wine of earth,

to body and blood of heaven;
our frail flesh and blood
to your holy people,
that we might be Christ's body to your world.

For this world we now pray:
end all war,
mend your wounded earth,
heal those who suffer,
comfort those who mourn,
and infuse us with your peace that is rooted in what is just.

Through the power of your Spirit unite us with Christ
and with one another
as we work and wait in hope,
confident in that day
when Christ will come to make all things well
and we will feast together at his heavenly table.

All glory and honor are yours, Holy God,
through Christ and in the unity of the Spirit,
now and forever. **Amen.**

ALL SAINTS

The Lord be with you.
And also with you.
Lift up your hearts.
We lift them to the Lord.
Let us give thanks to the Lord our God.
It is right to give our thanks and praise.

Gracious and Holy God,
you created the heavens and the earth
and all that is in them.
We praise you for you are our maker!   *Ps. 149:1–2*
We praise you for taking pleasure in your people
and lifting up the humble.   *Ps. 149:4*
In all ages, you have been faithful to us,
even when we were not faithful to you.
You have sent prophets and witnesses
to call us back to you when we ourselves grew weary,
stumbled, or fell from your way.
We recall some of their names before you in gratitude:
Abraham and Sarah, Moses and Miriam,
Isaiah, Ezekiel, and Daniel,
Elizabeth and Mary, Simeon and Anna,
Peter and James and John,
Mary and Martha,
Stephen, Paul, and Timothy,
Tabitha and Cornelius.

And we also recall those witnesses whose names are not recorded:
shepherds and magi,
a boy with loaves and fishes,
a little girl raised from the dead,
a man born blind, a woman whose back was bent,
the prodigal son, the Samaritan woman,
the rich young ruler, the widow with one coin,
unnamed women, the Ethiopian eunuch,
and countless more.

Out of your great love, you sent One who was more than witness:
Jesus Christ, your only Son, our Savior.
Born of Mary, he lived among us,
sharing our joys and our sorrows,
even suffering the pains of death.
By your power at work in Christ,   *Eph. 1:20*
he was raised from the dead
and is now seated at your right hand in the heavenly places,
above every name that is named,
not only in this age but also in the age to come.   *Eph. 1:21*

Gracious God,
by the power of your Holy Spirit,
help us to set our hope on Christ   *Eph. 1:12*
and live for the praise of his glory.
Pour out your Spirit upon us,
as you have poured out your Spirit
on generations past,
so that our love for all the saints might increase,   *Eph. 1:15*
and also our love for the world you love.
May the bread we break and the cup we bless
be for us the communion of the body and blood of Christ,
until that day,
until that great and promised day,
when we will feast with all the saints
in your eternal realm.
Through Christ, with Christ, in Christ,
in the unity of the Holy Spirit,
all glory and honor are yours, one God forever and ever. **Amen.**

REIGN OF CHRIST

The Lord be with you.
And also with you.
Lift up your hearts.
We lift them to the Lord.
Let us give thanks to the Lord, our God.
It is right to give our thanks and praise.

It is right that we praise you, Almighty God,
for you are without beginning and without end,
the source of all that exists.
Out of the darkness of chaos you brought forth creation
    in its abundance
through your eternal Son, Christ our Lord.
He is the visible image of your invisible glory and the
    firstborn of creation.
Through him you created heaven and earth,
and in him all things hold together in love.
With the thrones, dominions, rulers, and powers
    who live in joyful obedience to Christ
and with the angels and archangels and the
    hosts of heaven,
we join in the eternal song of praise: *Col. 1:15–20*

Holy, holy, holy Lord, God of power and might,
heaven and earth are full of your glory.
Hosanna in the highest.

Blessed is the One who comes in the name of the Lord.
Hosanna in the highest.

Holy are you and blessed is your Son, Jesus Christ.
He is the head of the church,
through whom you were pleased to reconcile to yourself all things,
whether on earth or in heaven.
Through his death he destroyed death
and through his resurrection and ascension he opened to all the way
    of your saving grace.
On the night he was betrayed,
he took bread, and when he had given thanks,
he broke it and gave it to them, saying,
This is my body, which is given for you.
Do this in remembrance of me.
And he did the same with the cup after supper, saying,
This cup that is poured out for you is the new covenant in my blood.
Do this in remembrance of me.

Remembering his life and suffering, his resurrection and ascension,
we offer our praise and thanksgiving for life with Christ.

Send your Holy Spirit upon us and upon this meal,
the bread of life and the cup of salvation.
Make us the body of Christ for the world,
a sign of your reign, which shall have no end.
Through your Son, Jesus Christ with the Holy Spirit,
all honor and glory are yours, Almighty God,
now and forever. **Amen.**

Scripture Index